THE KNOWLEDGE LIBRARY

DINOSAURS
and other
PREHISTORIC
ANIMALS

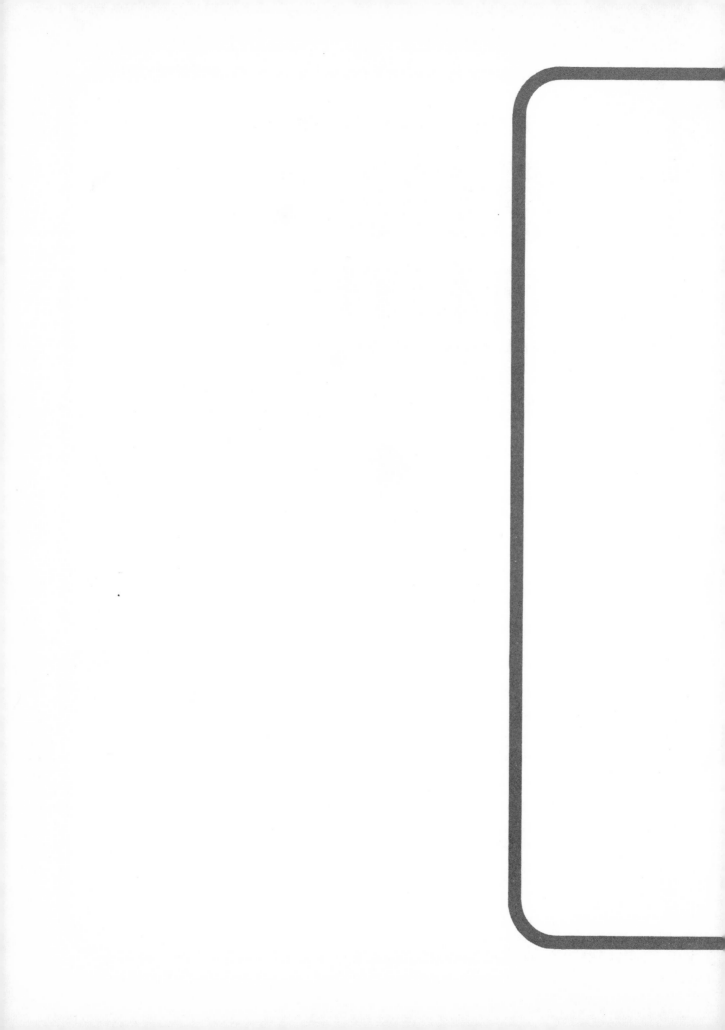

THE KNOWLEDGE LIBRARY

DINOSAURS and other PREHISTORIC ANIMALS

By Alfred Leutscher

Illustrated by Design Practitioners Ltd

GROSSET & DUNLAP

Publishers · NEW YORK
A National General Company

Published in the United States of America by
Grosset & Dunlap, Inc. New York, N.Y.

FIRST PRINTING 1971
Copyright © 1969, 1971 by The Hamlyn Publishing Group, Ltd.
All Rights Reserved.
Adapted from the Grosset All-Color Guide: PREHISTORIC ANIMALS
Library of Congress Catalog Card Number: 73-154875
ISBN: 0–448–00365–1 (Trade Edition)
ISBN: 0–448–07259–9 (Library Edition)
Printed by Officine Grafiche Arnoldo Mondadori, Verona, Italy.

contents

WHAT IS A FOSSIL?

This book is about prehistoric animals – how they have been preserved and what we have learned about them and their habits. Their remains are called fossils, a Latin word meaning "dug up," from the fact that they are found buried in the earth's crust beneath our feet.

Fossils are all around us. We can sometimes see shells or other remains of preserved animals as part of the stones we use for buildings. Fossils may be found on the sides of clay pits or in stone or limestone quarries. We can sometimes also find them along the sides of cliffs near the beach.

Over the past 250 years many interested people, including schoolchildren, have been searching for

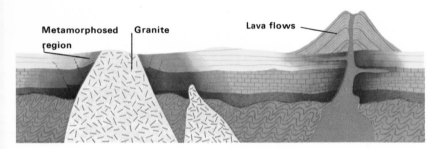

Metamorphosed region | Granite | Lava flows

fossils. A tooth here, a shell there, sometimes even whole skeletons have been found for us to see and study. Our museums and universities are full of these prehistoric treasures.

The study of fossils, called paleontology (pay-lee-on-tol-o-gee), can seem dull if you do not understand its true value. Fossils are the exciting clues to our story that begins with the first backboned fish of nearly 500 million years ago, and tells how, over hundreds of millions of years, amphibians, reptiles, birds, mammals and, finally, man, appeared and took their place in the animal kingdom that we know today.

Below left: In this section of the earth's crust we see layers of sedimentary rocks through which lava has forced its way up from a volcano. It will flow over the top and harden into igneous rock. In this way a volcanic mountain is built up.

On the left is the hardened rock of some ancient volcano which has turned into granite, a common igneous rock. Around it, the sedimentary rocks have been changed by heat and pressure to form metamorphic rock.

If we decided to search for fossils in this part of the earth's crust, we would avoid the volcanic areas, and instead approach the undisturbed sedimentary rocks somewhere in the middle of the picture. Depending on the age of the top layer, colored yellow, the fossils we might discover could be anything from fish to mammals.

Left: This river is slowly wearing down the mountains and carrying particles into the lake. One day the lake will become filled with sediment which will then harden into rock. The islands in the picture are already beginning to form on top of the lake where the sediment has reached the surface. In this way a whole sea may fill up to form sedimentary rock.

If any dead animals or plants should happen to sink to the bottom, their remains could get buried in the sediment and turn into fossils.

A FOSSIL GRAVEYARD

When looking for fossils it is of little use to go off and start to dig just anywhere. Fossils only turn up in certain kinds of rock, so it helps to know where they occur and how they are made. In the earth's crust there are three main kinds of rock. One of them, called *igneous*, meaning "fire," comes out of the interior, as lava and ash during a volcanic eruption. Since these rocks come from deep inside the earth, they never contain fossils.

When lava forces its way through the earth's crust, tremendous heat and pressure changes the character of the surrounding rocks. These are then called *metamorphic*, meaning "changed in form." They are usually hard and slaty, and split into sheets, and any contained fossils will be destroyed.

The third kind of rock is best for fossils. It is called *sedimentary*, meaning "laid down," and is formed in water. Over great periods of time land is worn away by rain, frost, wind and running water. Tiny particles are broken off and carried down to the sea or lakes by streams and rivers.

Slowly, these particles sink to the bottom of the sea and, in time, the sea may fill up and the particles harden into rock. So fossil-bearing, sedimentary rock can be soft or hard, smooth or rough, depending on the rock particles it is made from.

Below: This section of the earth's crust shows different layers of sedimentary rock, one on top of the other. In each layer different kinds of fossils may be found belonging to different ages. The rocks do not usually remain in flat layers, in such a neat and tidy fashion, however.

The earth's crust can be upset in many ways so that the rock layers get worn down or twisted and broken up. Sometimes rocks are folded and split, and may even be turned upside-down. This can pose a real puzzle for the paleontologist, who must then work out the position and age of each rock he examines. Only then will he know what fossils he might expect to find.

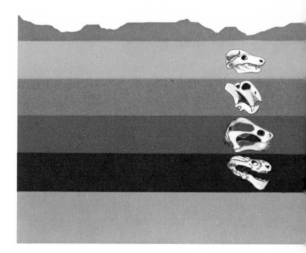

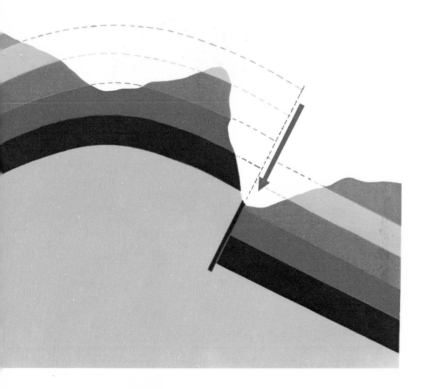

Left: Here we see a section of the earth's crust and what has happened to it over the ages. The dotted line shows the original outline of the sedimentary rocks. On the left, two things have happened. The rocks have been worn away to form a great hollow. This could be the work of a river as it slowly eats into the crust to form its valley. All the parts it has worn away will end in the sea to form a new layer of sedimentary rock. Also, these rocks have become curved due to some great pressure.

On the right, where the black arrow is pointing, the rock layers have split and slipped out of place. This is called a fault.

Faults are one of the hazards of mining. Digging along a seam of coal or gold, miners may come up against a blank wall. They will then have to search for the next layer of coal which may be much deeper, or higher, depending upon the slippage.

DATING THE ROCKS

A paleontologist can tell the age of each rock layer by radio-carbon dating. Certain rocks contain radio-active material which is breaking down slowly and steadily. For instance, uranium finally breaks down into lead. By measuring the amount of radio-active material in the rock a scientist can work out its age. If the rock contains fossils, he then knows how long ago each animal lived.

This connection between rocks and fossils was discovered by a British engineer, William Smith, while he was digging canals during the eighteenth century. He noticed that a certain fossil occurred in one kind of rock, but not in another. This was explained by the great naturalist Charles Darwin, in his Theory of Evolution. Different animals have lived at different times in the past, then have either died out so that others could take their place or have very slowly changed into another kind of animal.

Above: Limestone rock is usually pale in color and composed of very fine grains. It is a good rock in which to find fossils. The piece shown contains some shells.

EVOLUTION

In 1858 Charles Darwin announced his famous theory. He explained how life is always changing, because the world around us is changing, too. He called life a "struggle for existence," where animals and plants are always competing with one another for food and living space. In this struggle only the successful forms of life manage to survive.

Plants and animals have adapted themselves to their surroundings. For example, a woodpecker is suited to living in trees, a fish to a pond, and a polar bear to the cold Arctic. If the trees disappear, the pond dries up or the Arctic climate becomes warm, then these three animals no longer fit in. They may die out unless they can evolve into something which will suit their new environment.

Throughout the ages climates have changed, mountains have been built and worn away, seas have changed places with the land, and life itself

Above: This is coal. It is not a true rock, but was created from ancient plants that after death have been compressed. Most coal formation took place in the Carboniferous period.

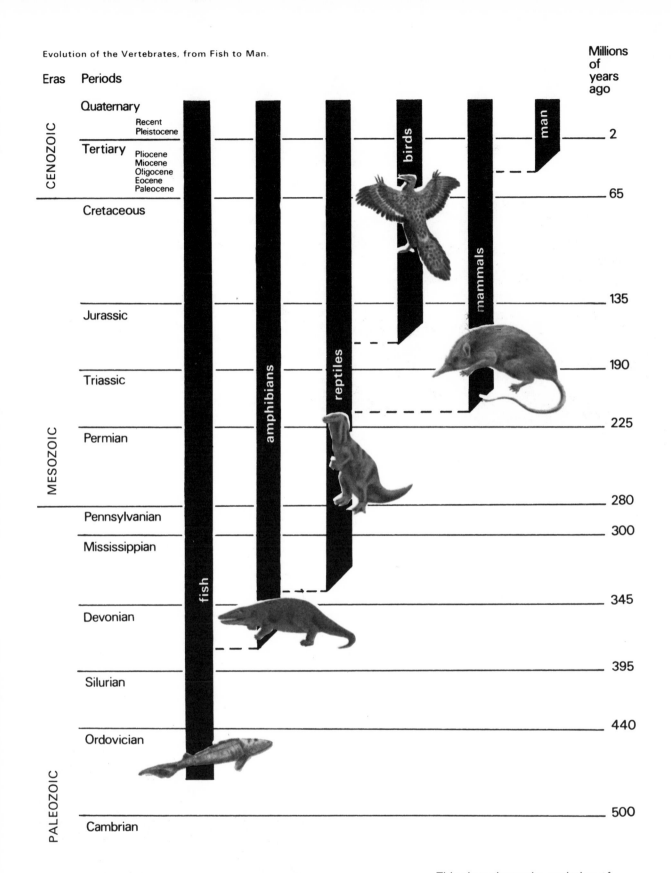

Evolution of the Vertebrates, from Fish to Man.

Eras — **Periods** — **Millions of years ago**

Eras	Periods	
CENOZOIC	Quaternary	Recent / Pleistocene
	Tertiary	Pliocene / Miocene / Oligocene / Eocene / Paleocene
	Cretaceous	
MESOZOIC	Jurassic	
	Triassic	
	Permian	
	Pennsylvanian	
	Mississippian	
	Devonian	
PALEOZOIC	Silurian	
	Ordovician	
	Cambrian	

Millions of years ago: 2, 65, 135, 190, 225, 280, 300, 345, 395, 440, 500

Labels on chart: man, birds, mammals, reptiles, amphibians, fish

This chart shows the evolution of vertebrates. On the left are the names of the earth's periods, with the oldest at the bottom. On the right are the dates in millions of years when these periods existed.

Right: A mammoth has been trapped in a swamp. If it cannot escape, it will drown. It could also turn into a fossil. In places like Alaska and Siberia, where the ground is always frozen, mammoths and woolly rhinoceroses have been found with skin and hair still attached to their bodies.

Left: Here are the remains of a mammoth which lived during the Ice Age and died about ten thousand years ago. It has been uncovered by a paleontologist and appears to be in good condition. Most of the bones, as well as the tusks, are in position. Now the long task will begin to remove it from the surrounding matrix. Usually mammoths are buried in soft clay, so the work should not be too difficult.

As each bone is removed, it will be packed away in a box with a label and numbered before it is transported to a museum.

has had to change as well. In this book we shall follow one of the main branches of life. It starts with fish and continues up to ourselves – man. All of these creatures have one thing in common, a backbone. We call them vertebrates.

DIGGING UP FOSSILS

Most fossils are formed under water. A lifeless body on land soon decomposes or gets eaten by another animal. If it sinks to the bottom of the sea or a lake, however, the sediment covers it up so that the hard parts are held together. It is usually only the bones, teeth and shells of animals that remain preserved in the rocks. Only rarely is there a footprint or the imprint of the skin to be found.

Finding fossils takes time. First, you must know where to look. Then, when the fossil is found, it must be removed carefully and brought to a laboratory to be cleaned and studied by paleontologists.

Right: This paleontologist is putting the finishing touches to a fossil skeleton. It shows the backbone and skull, and one or two bones alongside. He may decide to remove it from the rock, or leave it just as it died.

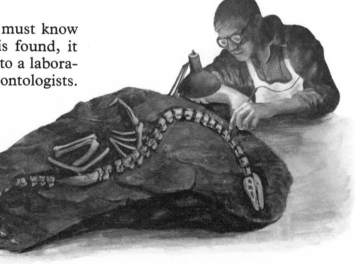

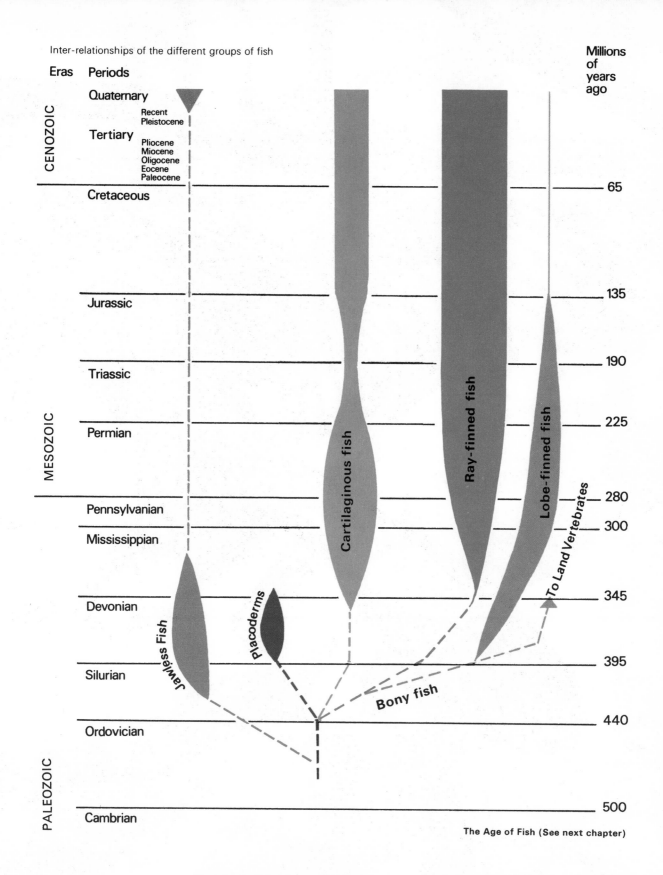

Inter-relationships of the different groups of fish

| Eras | Periods | | Millions of years ago |

Eras · Periods

Millions of years ago

CENOZOIC

Quaternary
Recent
Pleistocene

Tertiary
Pliocene
Miocene
Oligocene
Eocene
Paleocene

Cretaceous — 65

MESOZOIC

Jurassic — 135

Triassic — 190

Permian — 225

Pennsylvanian — 280

Mississippian — 300

Devonian — 345

Silurian — 395

Ordovician — 440

PALEOZOIC

Cambrian — 500

Cartilaginous fish

Ray-finned fish

Lobe-finned fish

To Land Vertebrates

Jawless Fish

Placoderms

Bony fish

The Age of Fish (See next chapter)

Overleaf: This picture shows a reconstruction of the world of that most famous of fossil finds, *Archaeopteryx*, the bird-lizard. Pterosaurs, true flying lizards, are gliding from the trees to scoop up fish in their long beaks.

Archaeopteryx's skeleton, found in a limestone quarry near Solnhofen in Germany, is important because it shows the development of flying lizards into birds.

FISH—THE FIRST VERTEBRATES

We now begin the exciting story of life in which, over many millions of years, backboned animals have evolved from small, primitive, fish-like creatures into the newest and latest of vertebrates – ourselves. Along the way we will learn, in the order in which they appeared, something of the amphibians, the reptiles, the birds, and the mammals.

Bringing prehistoric animals "back to life" is not easy, and we shall never know some of their characteristics. We do not know for example, what color they were or what sounds they made. It is easier to find out what they fed on by looking at their teeth. We can tell from the shape and the types of leg they had whether they walked, hopped, ran, flew or swam, and we can compare them with similar animals that are alive today.

Below: Here are two more ostracoderm fish. The top one, *Hemicyclaspis*, was about eight inches long. It had simple fins on either side of its head. The rows of muscles seen underneath (in the cutaway view) are important to fish because they help to swing the body and tail from side to side when swimming. Fins are utilized to maintain balance. The backbone is along the top.

The fish below it is *Thelodus*, of about the same size. Instead of having a covering of bony armor, the skin is full of tiny scales. Some scientists think that these scales are found only in young specimens, so this one may only be a youngster.

THE OSTRACODERMS

The first vertebrates to appear were fish called ostracoderms. Most of them had a heavy armor of bone around their head and the front part of their body, and thick scales over the rest. Unlike later fish, they had mouths without moving jaws, and there were no paired fins on their bodies.

These primitive fish could not have been very active. Many of them had flattened bodies, so it is probable that they rested on the water bottom and fed by sifting through the mud.

Above left: These small ostracoderms show their bony armor on the front part of their bodies. The upper one is called *Pteraspis*, about six inches long, and looks as if it was a lively little fish. *Drepanaspis* (below) about twelve inches long, had a flattened body and a rounded, wide mouth. It probably lived on the water bottom and sifted through the mud for food.

Ostracoderms are found all over the world. They mostly lived in the Devonian period, in either freshwater or the sea.

THE PLACODERMS

By the time the Devonian period began, ostracoderms were joined by other primitive fish called placoderms, meaning "plated skins." They also had bony armor on their bodies in many cases, but differed from ostracoderms in that they had movable jaws with teeth, and paired fins like modern fish. Of the four fish pictured below, *Dinichthys* was a giant. It reached a length of 30 feet and its powerful jaws could easily have crushed smaller armored fish. Slender *Acanthodes*, about 12 inches long, existed longer than any of the other placoderms, right into the Permian period, and *Bothiolepis*, pictured at the bottom of the page, had a pair of jointed "arms" behind its head that may have been used for walking in the same way that a lobster uses its legs.

Above left: A modern lamprey called *Petromyzon*. It has a sucker for a mouth instead of jaws, and a tongue covered with horny teeth.

Above right: *Pharyngolepis,* about seven inches long, was a jawless fish which could have been an ancestor of the modern lamprey.

THE LAMPREY

Apart from clumsy and slow-moving ostracoderms, there were other such fish with more slender bodies. They would have been far more active, and could probably dart about catching smaller fish, or wriggle into the mud and holes in the rocks to escape from enemies. It is these slender kinds that have lived and evolved to this day.

In rivers and lakes, as well as the sea, there are some strange creatures called lampreys and hagfish that are still in existence. They have no jaws or paired fins, and are supposed to be the descendants of the ancient ostracoderms. The dotted line of the chart on page 11 shows that jawless fish therefore are thought to have survived from the Silurian period to the present day.

Left: (top to bottom) *Dinichthys, Climatius, Acanthodes* and *Bothiolepis.* Tiny *Climatius,* about three inches long, had paired fins and a row of single fins along its underside.

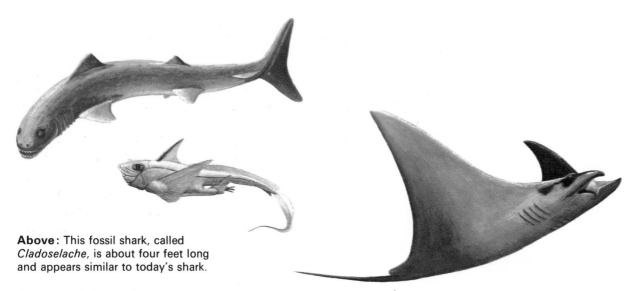

Above: This fossil shark, called *Cladoselache*, is about four feet long and appears similar to today's shark.

Center: This is a present-day cartilaginous fish called *Chimaera*, a deep-sea fish with a pointed snout and a whip-like tail. It feeds on shell fish. We are not certain of the specific ancestors of this strange fish.

Above right: This is the world's largest ray, called the manta or devil fish. Its length ranges up to twenty-one feet, and the enormous spread of its "wings" can be up to twenty-four feet across. It swims majestically through warm seas with slow beats of its fins, and sometimes frightens divers, though it is quite harmless.

Right: This map of part of the world shows where most of the Devonian fish have been found. Their fossils are usually buried in a sandstone rock which was built up in lakes and seas in very warm times. When the lakes dried up, many fish were trapped in the mud and preserved there. The red sandstone rock in the county of Devon, England, where these fish were first discovered, is a good example of this period.

CARTILAGINOUS FISH

Today, these fish consist of the sharks, skates and rays. The special thing about them is that their skeletons are made of gristle, a much softer substance than bone, and called cartilage. The only hard parts are the teeth and the tiny pointed scales in the skin. As a result, these fish have not fossilized well in the past, and in some cases a prehistoric shark is only known from preserved teeth. Sharks are active hunters, beautifully streamlined, and sometimes dangerous to man. They vary in size from a small dogfish about three feet long, to the world's largest

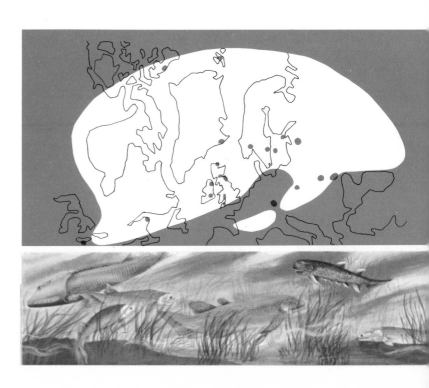

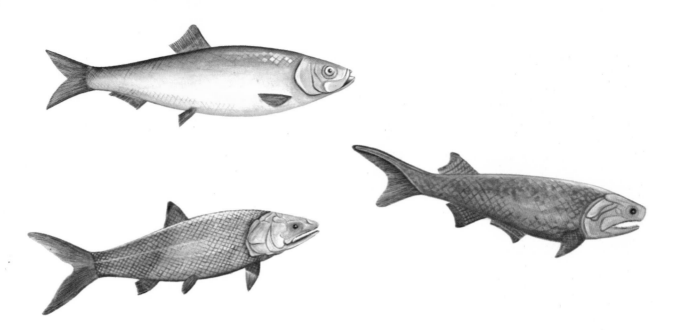

Above: *Clupea,* a modern herring.

Left: *Caturus,* an ancient ray-finned fish which did not look so very different from the herring.

Right: *Cheirolepis* lived in the Devonian seas. It had thick scales and solid fins.

Left: Shown here are fish in a warm Devonian lake. Placoderms and ostracoderms were common during this period. On the far left is *Hemicyclaspis,* an ostracoderm, and on the far right is *Climatius,* an early jawed fish. Whole "graveyards" of fossil fish have been discovered in the mud of dried-up lakes which have turned into stone.

fish today, a shark called the Whale Shark. It can grow up to 14 yards. Even so, there may have been prehistoric sharks up to 30 yards long, judging by their teeth. Some of them, though, were only six inches long.

Skates and rays are built quite differently from sharks, and usually live on the sea bed. A skate is a kind of flattened dogfish with enormous front fins looking like a pair of wings. When the skate swims, these wing-like fins make a beautiful wavy movement.

THE BONY FISHES – THE RAY-FINS

Beside the cartilaginous fish, there is another big group of advanced fish called bony fish because of their bony skeletons. One of their major subdivisions consists of the ray-fins. The ray-finned fish have bony struts arranged like a fan inside their fins.

Nearly all the bony fish living today belong to this group. They swarm in the seas, rivers and lakes all over the world, and provide us with food. The cod, herring, sole and salmon are examples. One of their most successful adaptations is the swim bladder. Cartilaginous fish do not have one. The air in their bladder can be altered in balance with the changing pressure of the water outside the fish. A fish thus can "hang" motionless in the water instead of sinking or floating to the surface. It need not waste its energy. The swim bladder adjusts itself to each pressure.

Clupea, the modern herring, pictured above, is a ray-finned bony fish. It is about eight inches long and is a valuable food fish that swims about in shoals.

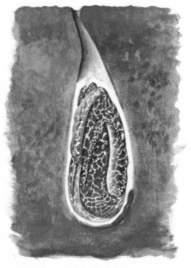

Left: The African lungfish called *Protopterus* has a slender body and tentacle-like fins. When its home dries up, it burrows into the mud and forms a hard cocoon which has a small opening at the ground surface. There it is safe from enemies and can actually breathe air. When the rainy season begins and the lake fills up, the lungfish breaks out of its shelter and returns to living like a fish. Lungfish have sharp teeth and hunt other water animals.

THE LOBE-FINS

We now come to a group of bony fish that form an important link in our story. They were not as successful as the ray-fins, but some became the ancestors of the first land vertebrates, called amphibians.

The shape of their fins was very interesting. Instead of spreading out like a fan, as in the ray-fins, each of their paired lobe-shaped fins had a row of bones running down the center. It was these fins that turned into an arm or leg with fingers and toes.

One kind of lobe-fin alive today is the famous coelacanth, called *Latimeria*, shown here. It appeared in a fisherman's catch one day, after

everyone thought that it had become extinct.

Other kinds of lobe-fins, called lungfish, which also lived during the Devonian period are still alive today. It seems that all lobe-fins, including the extinct forms, had air-breathing lungs as well as gills.

If a fish leaves the water and evolves into a land animal, there are two main things that it needs – a pair of lungs for breathing and legs for walking. This change from lobe-finned fish to the first land vertebrate occurred during the late Devonian period.

Left: Here is the only surviving coelacanth. It is found in the deep waters around the east coast of South Africa, in the Indian Ocean. Note the remarkable lobe-shaped fins which are on stalks, unlike the fan-shaped fins of modern ray-finned fish.

Right through their long history, coelacanths have changed little in appearance. Some years ago a paleontologist examined a fossil coelacanth over 70 million years old, and made a model of it. When the modern coelacanth was discovered it looked almost exactly the same as the constructed replica.

The average size of a modern coelacanth is about five feet. The skin is a shiny, metal-blue when the fish is still alive.

Above: Of all the lobe fins, those like this one, called *Eusthenopteron*, are the most likely ancestors of the amphibians. Their skeletons were similar, as were their teeth, which were strong and covered with a hard enamel, a substance which is also on our teeth.

Eusthenopteron and his cousins had died out by the beginning of the Permian period. Long before then, during the late Devonian period, to be exact, certain of the lobe fins had begun to crawl onto the land. These became the first vertebrates with five-fingered limbs. They are called amphibians.

THE COELACANTH

Until 1938, it was thought from their fossils that coelacanths lived from the Devonian period to the Cretaceous period, an enormous length of time.

Then, in 1938, some fishermen caught a live coelacanth at East London, a town on the Indian Ocean in South Africa. It soon died. Fortunately, the curator of a nearby museum, Miss Courtney Latimer, who was called down to see it, recognized it as an important discovery, and saved the remains.

Later, a marine scientist, Professor Smith, examined this fish and gave it a name. He named it after Miss Latimer, and so it is now known as *Latimeria*. Since then, other coelacanths have been caught, but none have managed to live, even though they were kept in tanks of sea water. It may be that because they live in deep water they cannot survive in shallow water under bright daylight.

It is seemingly incredible that these fish have been living on earth for over 300 million years, when we thought that they had died out long ago. The marine coelacanths are thought to be descended from fresh-water lobe-fin ancestors.

CONTINENTAL DRIFT

We have just learned of some of the "living fossils" that are scattered around the world. They have lived unchanged for millions of years, such as the lobe-fins, some of which are still here today. Later on, we shall learn of others. What is puzzling to many scientists is that such specimens have been found in widespread places. Lungfish, for example, are found in South America, Africa and Australia – with miles of ocean in between.

One theory to explain this is that the continents were once joined together long ago, but that slowly, they were torn apart and drifted away from each other. Underneath the earth's crust is a vast layer of half-liquid rock on which the continents are floating. It is as if mankind were living on huge rafts, some people on one and some people on others. If this theory is correct then this would explain why the lungfish and other living fossils are now so widely spread out. It is interesting to look at a world map, and to see that in many places the coastlines would fit into each other very neatly.

AMPHIBIANS – THE HALFWAY ANIMALS

EARLY AMPHIBIANS

As the Devonian period came to an end, a number of primitive amphibians began to appear. The word *amphibia* is Greek for "two lives," and was given to them because, as babies, they grow up in water. We call these babies tadpoles. They take oxygen from the water by means of gills and swim with their tails. Next legs grow and lungs for breathing air take the place of gills. Now they are ready to live on land. We think this is how certain lobe-fin fish evolved into amphibians.

Amphibians, then, needed lungs to breathe air and limbs with which to walk on land. Lobe-finned fish already had both these requirements fairly well developed, and so they were the ones to crawl out of the swamps during the Coal Age.

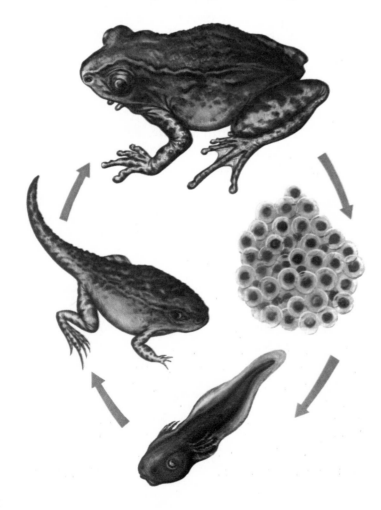

Left: This frog is a modern amphibian. Like toads, frogs go through a kind of "double life," starting with eggs laid in water. When the eggs are laid by the female, each one is covered with a protective coat of jelly. In some amphibians the eggs are massed together in clumps of spawn; in others they are laid in long strings. The eggs then hatch into babies which extract oxygen from the water by means of gills.

Using their tails, they swim about in search of food. Most of the tadpoles of frogs and toads feed on water plants, and may be kept in an aquarium. It is interesting to watch their daily growth. As the gills disappear, the growing amphibians develop lungs and legs. Then one day they hop out of the water as young frogs and toads.

Baby newts and salamanders also have gills. They usually feed on small water animals that can hardly be seen.

Left: *Ichthyostega*, the earliest known amphibian. It lived in the swamps of the late Devonian period which were rapidly disappearing owing to the very dry climate. The strange plants that grew in these swamps are the earliest known land plants. They did not have flowers and many of them crept along the ground to grow new shoots.

At the end of this period, most of the ostracoderms and placoderms had died out. A few of the lobe-fin fish, such as the lung-fish and the coelacanth managed to live on and give rise to the amphibians.

Other changes necessary for life on land are a stronger backbone to support the body, eardrums to hear sounds coming through the air, and eyelids to protect the eyes. These features are present in amphibians today.

There are exceptions, of course. Certain salamanders and frogs stay in the water all their lives, having become more aquatic than their ancestors.

AN EARLY AMPHIBIAN – ICHTHYOSTEGA

Above there is one of the earliest known amphibians, *Ichthyostega*. It was about three feet long, and had a powerful tail with a fin along the border. This made it a good swimmer, like its lobe-fin ancestors. At the same time, it had legs for walking and nostrils leading into the mouth. Fossils of this amphibian, which lived during the late Devonian period, have been found in Greenland. In those days that region was very much warmer than it is today, and the vegetation was tropical.

Only a few remains of *Ichthyostega* have been found, and a lot more remains to be discovered about this first amphibian. We do know, however, that *Ichthyostega* had five digits on each foot. Since all vertebrates today are descended from these amphibians, this explains why ten fingers and ten toes are the standard equipment for all vertebrates. The exceptions that do exist are in animals that have lost some of these digits in the course of evolution.

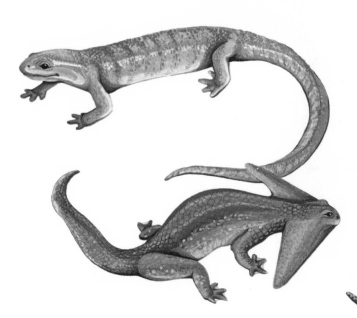

Left: *Cardiocephalus*, about five inches long, looks like a modern salamander.

Below: *Diplocaulus* was two feet long and had a peculiar arrow-shaped head.

Above: *Microbrachis* is another Carboniferous salamander.

THE COAL AGE

By the time of the Carboniferous period, amphibians were dominating the swamps and marshy places of the earth. The Devonian ostracoderm and placoderm fish had all disappeared by then.

In the seas, sharks and rays were in command. In fresh water, the ray-fins were increasing, but the lobe-fins were far fewer in number.

This period is sometimes called the Coal Age. It is divided into the Lower Carboniferous, or Mississipian period, and the Upper Carboniferous, or Pennsylvanian period. Most of the fresh water animals, such as amphibians, come from the Pennsylvanian period, when many of the coal deposits were being formed.

In those days there were giant, fast growing trees which formed the great swamp forests in which the amphibians lived. Some of them, called club-mosses, grew up to a hundred feet tall and had scaly bark. Others, like the giant horsetails, grew up to thirty feet tall, and looked very much like the small horsetail plants of today.

On the floor of the steamy swamps grew masses of ferns. All of these ancient plants are shown in the scene of a Coal Age forest on the right.

This was the home of the first amphibians, creatures that crawled over the mud, but could also swim in the water. They laid their eggs in water and occasionally small fossils of youngsters have been found with traces of gills.

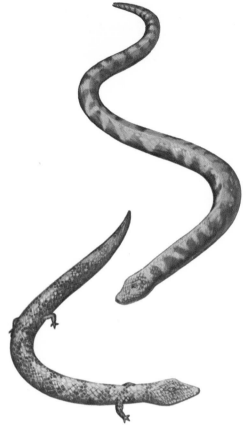

The amphibians of today are broadly of two kinds. There are the frogs and toads which can hop and swim with their hind feet that have webs between the toes. They have no tails. Then there are the newts and salamanders which have slender bodies, weak legs, but strong tails for swimming. There is a third group, not very well known, of worm-like burrowing amphibians, called coecilians or apodals.

In the past, most of the early amphibians were of the salamander kind, and varied from a few inches to up to nine or twelve feet long.

Whereas some early amphibians had parts of their backs and sides covered with bony scales, like their fish ancestors, all modern frogs and salamanders are naked – only the coecilians have a few tiny scales. This naked skin serves a very useful purpose. It permits oxygen to enter through the pores, thus serving as a kind of lung surface. However, because their skins are naked, amphibians have to stay in damp surroundings to avoid drying out.

Above: Here are two Coal Age amphibians with slender bodies. On the left is *Sauropleura*, about eight inches long, which probably lived only in the water. On the right is *Ophiderpeton*, about two feet long. It had no legs and was probably a burrower in the mud, like the coecilians of today.

TOWARD THE REPTILES

By the end of the Coal Age some amphibians, probably the ancestors of the reptiles, began to appear. Their skeletons were built along reptilian lines, and a number of them had scaly skins, too.

One very important difference distinguishes these two vertebrates. As we have already learned, amphibians grow up in water as tadpoles – from eggs that are laid in water – and they have gills at first.

Reptiles, on the other hand, always lay their eggs on land, even though some of them live most of their lives in water – as turtles do. There is no gilled stage in the young. This is possible because a reptile's egg is enclosed in a shell, and can be laid on land. The baby reptile develops inside the egg.

An animal called *Seymouria* is shown on the right. *Seymouria* comes from within the land area that is now the United States, and was about two feet long. It was a land-living vertebrate that resembled a reptile in many but not all respects.

Diadectes was another amphibian so similar in construction to a reptile that at first it was classified that way. Now it has been put in with the amphibians because of certain critical features of the skeleton that had not been studied earlier.

The essential point that separates amphibians from reptiles is their reproductive habit. And, of course, it is very difficult to determine this from fossil material. The very first fossil "land" egg, one that certainly belonged to a reptile, has been found in a sedimentary deposit laid down during the Permian period. But this does not mean that vertebrates laying shelled eggs had not evolved before that time. Both *Seymouria* and *Diadectes* are "in between" kinds of creature, to judge from their skeletons. They appear in deposits that already contain full-fledged reptiles, so they cannot have been their ancestors. *Seymouria* and *Diadectes* are important because they disclose what the amphibian ancestors of the reptile must have looked like.

Left: This large amphibian, called *Eryops*, grew up to six feet in length, had a leathery skin containing a few scales, and moved about slowly and clumsily on land. It may also have entered the water to search for food, in the way that a crocodile does today.

One of the largest of present-day amphibians is the giant salamander *Megalobatrachus*, found in the rivers of China and Japan. Like *Eryops*, it has sharp teeth for catching fish. By keeping very still underwater it can surprise its prey, should it come too close, then suddenly pounce. The giant salamander is sometimes caught for food.

Above: *Archeria* was nearly six feet long and had a webbed tail. It probably swam much of the time and may have hunted fish and other, smaller amphibians. Below it is *Seymouria*, which was much more reptile-like in structure, and lived mostly on land.

Below right: Two North American salamanders. There are many kinds in the United States and they can make interesting pets.

You need a glass enclosure in which mosses and small ferns can grow, so that it looks like a miniature garden. Stones and broken flowerpots will make "hiding places." This home must be kept damp, and will need a dish of water as a "pond." The salamanders may lay eggs in it. Some of them, called newts, will stay for many months in water, and would do better in an aquarium. If the eggs hatch and turn into baby salamanders, you can watch them grow up. They will need feeding on tiny water animals which can be caught in a pond with a fine net.

At first they breathe with gills and have no legs. Then the legs appear and lungs take the place of gills, until they are ready to crawl out. Altogether this development takes about twelve weeks. It is like watching a condensed drama of what happened millions of years ago, when fish slowly evolved into amphibians and became land animals.

MODERN SALAMANDERS

Below are two modern salamanders found in North America. They are amphibians that mostly live in the Northern Hemisphere. By day they hide away to protect themselves from their enemies, but more especially to avoid the dry air and hot sun. Such exposure would damage their sensitive skins, dry them out, and kill them.

Salamanders never seem to be in a hurry. People sometimes confuse them with lizards, which are very lively. Lizards are reptiles, have scales on their bodies, and like to bask in the sunshine.

A salamander protects itself with a very evil-tasting liquid inside its skin. If an enemy grabs one, it will probably drop it in a hurry, and it is not likely to make the same mistake twice.

The European fire salamander has the interesting habit of bearing its young alive. Instead of laying jelly-covered eggs into the water, the female gives birth to wriggling larval salamanders.

Right: This is *Kotlassia*, an amphibian with strong legs, which was beginning to look like a reptile. The smaller amphibian is the tiny *Discosauriscus*. It was only ten inches long, and was heavily scaled like a reptile, probably to give it some protection.

CONQUEST OF THE LAND

All through the Carboniferous period the amphibians predominated in the swamps and lakes.

Although they could live on land in some cases, they were not able to move far from water where the eggs had to be laid. This is still true today with most amphibians. If a pond dries up, then all the frogs, toads and salamanders must find another one in order to survive.

The real conquest of the land began in the Permian period, which followed the Coal Age, when animals began to lay eggs that were covered by a shell. Such an egg protects the baby inside, and it grows in a kind of "private pond."

This is what reptiles do, and that is why they can lay their eggs out of water. Inside, the baby reptile is bathed in a watery fluid, called albumen, and it even has a supply of food, called yolk. On the other hand, the tadpole, or larva, of an amphibian grows up in the open water, searching for its food and evading enemies. Enormous numbers get caught and eaten, whereas the baby reptiles are relatively safe inside their eggshells.

Such a shell-egg gets warmed by its surroundings. A reptile mother will bury her clutch of eggs in the soil or in rotting vegetation where there is enough heat to hatch them. Even though she does not protect or feed her young, as birds do, these babies are well able to look after themselves. They break out of their shells and immediately start looking for food.

Left: This is a scene from the Upper Permian period in South Africa, looking lush and tropical. In the Lower Permian period this part of the world was much colder, and there were glaciers, one of which is still filling up the mountain valley in the distance. Fossil reptiles have also turned up in this part of the world.

This meant that reptiles could now ignore the watery places and explore the dry land. This they did, and it was the beginning of a great invasion. More and more reptiles appeared and swarmed everywhere. They entered the forest and deserts, climbed trees, and even took to the air. But there were some that turned back to the water and lived in the seas.

This was the beginning of the Age of Reptiles which was to last for millions of years, culminating with the appearance of the dinosaurs, about which more later.

Reptiles have a system unlike that of birds and mammals when it comes to body temperature regulation. Birds and mammals are warm-blooded, but reptiles are cold-blooded. That means that the outside surroundings determine the internal temperature of the reptile's body. Many lizards, snakes, turtles and crocodiles will therefore bask in· the sun for hours to attain high enough body temperatures for them to become active for hunting and other bodily functions. Their scales prevent drying out and they can always seek the shade when they get too hot.

Above: This map shows the places where early reptiles have been found, such as North America, the Soviet Union, and South Africa.

Right: This is *Hylonomus*, one of the first reptiles.

THE FIRST REPTILES

Reptiles were beginning to appear in fair numbers during the Permian period. At first they were quite small, not measuring much more than twelve inches long. They were hunters and fed on insects and other small creatures. Some were very lizard-like such as *Hylonomus*, pictured above.

Although lizards are not related to ancient reptiles, they give us an idea of how they lived. Much of their time was spent basking in the sun, keeping quite still. Then when an insect moved nearby, the little reptile would dart at its prey, catching it in its mouth. These speedy movements also protected them from their enemies.

REPTILIAN PLANT-EATERS

Most of today's reptiles are hunters – they catch other animals for food. In the prehistoric past, however, quite a number of them were plant-eaters, especially the immense, bulky ones. During the Permian period some of these vegetarians appeared. Many of them were up to nine feet long and stood about five feet high. Their remains have been found in South Africa and Russia.

These clumsy plant-eaters were rather bowlegged and must have waddled about awkwardly in their swampy surroundings where plants were plentiful in the soft mud.

It is not at all unusual that the larger animals such as the elephant, cow, horse, etc., feed on plants. Plant material is not so easy to digest as meat, and so it stays in the body much longer before it is used up. A plant-eater needs to have a larger stomach and a longer intestine to take in more food and to digest it properly. A grass-eating rabbit, for example, has an intestine which is far longer than that of a meat-eating dog.

Left: *Hypsognathus*, one of the early reptiles, was about twelve inches long and a hunter of small animals.

This reptile was found in New Jersey, in Triassic deposits, and can be recognized by the bony spikes on the top and sides of its head. This may have given it some protection from enemies. The spines may have also protected the body from drying up by reflecting the hot sun.

Many lizards today that live in desert surroundings are spiny, just like the desert cactus. All forms of life must have water, and where it is hard to find, it must be saved and stored within the plant's or animal's body.

Left: This is the large, clumsy looking *Pareiasaurus,* about 3 feet long, a plant-eater. It lived among the swamps and was found in South America.

SHIP LIZARDS OR "SAIL-BACKS"

These two names are given to some early reptiles that have strange-looking fins, shaped like sails on their backs. They belong to the end of the Carboniferous and early part of the Permian period.

The reason for these sails is not certain. They consisted of a layer of skin stretched over a framework of bones, and may have helped to regulate the body temperature.

In some parts of the world where winters are especially cold, reptiles will hibernate. In other places, where it gets extremely hot and dry, they will also hide away. This is because reptiles are dependent on outside temperatures.

A sail-back could have made use of its sail by turning sideways to the sun and getting the fullest possible coverage from the rays. Then the creature would soon warm up. But if it faced the sun head-on, the rays' warmth would be minimal.

A bird will sometimes stretch out on the ground with its wings spread out to sunbathe. A lizard will lie on a warm stone and flatten its body to absorb the heat. Even a butterfly at rest on a flower will sometimes tilt sideways to the sun's rays.

The "sail-backs" and other reptiles like them, but without "sails," are considered the first mammal-like reptiles. This, then, is the beginning of a very varied range of reptiles, some of which eventually developed into true warm-blooded mammals.

Below: This is a well-known "sail-back" called *Dimetrodon*. It was an early mammal-like reptile about eleven feet long, and had a tall "sail." It was found in Texas, and had sharp meat-eating teeth.

Somebody once suggested that the sail was actually used to catch the wind when this reptile went into the water, and called it a "ship-lizard."

This seems doubtful, since swimming animals usually have webbed feet or a flat tail. *Dimetrodon* looks much more like a walking animal. Because of its size it must have been one of the most dominating meat-eaters of its time.

Right: *Edaphosaurus* had a sail, and looks a bit like *Dimetrodon*. It had special crushing teeth for feeding on shellfish, and lived in swampy places.

HERDS OF REPTILES

By the middle of the Permian period there were large numbers of other mammal-like reptiles living. Many of their remains have been found in South Africa, although they also occur on other continents.

Today South Africa is a dry country under a hot sun, so that the rocks are continually wearing away and crumbling. Hundreds of fossils of these ancient reptiles are found there every year.

It seems incredible that skeletons such as these may have been lying buried for some 200 million years, and then one day just appear on the surface for us to pick up.

The Permian reptiles pictured on this page lived on into the Triassic period in some cases, but then their time came to an end. Large and

Left: Two of the clumsy Permian dicynodonts. Above is the hippo-like *Lystrosaurus*, about three feet long, and below it the larger *Dinodontosaurus*, about six feet long.

Notice the sharp eye teeth, forming tusks, and also the horny beak, which might have been used for chopping off vegetation in the manner of present-day tortoises.

clumsy in many cases, they waddled about awkwardly on their bowlegs. Some were plant-eaters, others were hunters, like *Lycaenops*, pictured on the next page. Some had a pair of sharp, tusk-like teeth in the front of their upper jaws. They are called dicynodonts, (die-sigh-no-donts), meaning "double dog teeth." These reptiles were plant-eaters and the tusks served for defense.

There were many kinds of these bulky plant-eaters, which seemed to have mainly roamed in large herds on the dry plains of Africa. Although some were no bigger than a rabbit, others grew to the size of a rhinoceros. They had peg-like teeth which could be used for browsing on vegetation. Others had turtle-like beaks.

HUNTER AND HUNTED

It is interesting to compare the living and feeding habits of the ancient reptiles with other groups of animals. Millions of years ago, during the Permian period, fierce hunters like *Titanosuchus*, preyed on a clumsy plant-eater, *Moschops*, and set up a pattern that has never changed.

Millions of years later it was the dinosaur's turn, as we shall see. Then, even later, during the Age of Mammals, saber-toothed cats preyed on herds of plant-eating mammals.

Today it is very much the same. The lion hunts the zebra, the fox the rabbit, and the cat the mouse. Among reptiles the crocodile preys on animals which come down to the water to drink, and the python catches monkeys in the trees.

Above: Another hunter already quite mammalian in appearance, called *Lycaenops* and about three feet long. Its sharp eye teeth can clearly be seen.

Left: A battle between two advanced mammal-like reptiles: one a hunter, the other a plant-eater. The long-tailed attacker is *Titanosuchus*, a slim and powerful reptile, well able to catch the clumsy *Moschops* on the right. They were both about eight feet long.

It is important to understand this way of life, because this natural balance can be easily upset. By killing off too many hunting animals we cause the plant-eaters to increase, because we decrease the natural hazards they have to face. Then there is trouble as they eat up the grass and crops.

In North America, among other places, this has already happened. Where the jackal and puma once lived but are now gone, the deer and the prairie dog have become too numerous and are damaging the grass and trees.

On the opposite page is a map of the places where mammal-like reptiles from the Triassic period were found – mainly in South Africa and America, but also in parts of Europe. It is thought that in those days there was no Atlantic Ocean, and all the continents were joined together.

THE MAMMAL-LIKE REPTILES

Let us go into the reasons for having called the "sail-backs" and the other reptiles just discussed mammal-like reptiles.

One peculiar mammalian characteristic is the teeth. Usually reptiles only have one kind of tooth repeated all along the length of their jaws. However, the kind of tooth this is can vary. Snakes and crocodiles have sharp, curved teeth for catching their prey; some lizards, like iguanas, have blunt teeth for chewing plants; turtles have no teeth, they have a beak instead.

In mammals there are all sorts of teeth in the same jaw. Rodents like mice and squirrels have large chisel-like front teeth for nibbling at leaves, nuts and bark, while the back teeth are broad grinding mills. Hunters, such as lions and wolves, have large canines or eye teeth for stabbing into meat, and teeth built for slicing further back in the jaws. Plant-eating deer and cattle have especially broad back teeth good for grinding up vegetation.

Opposite: On the opposite page is a modern dog. This shows some of the mammal-like reptiles may have had dog-like teeth and were hunters, but they were still reptiles, and not really mammals. A true mammal has hair, and its babies are fed on milk. A reptile is scaly and usually lays eggs which it then ignores. Also, a mammal has constantly warm blood, whereas a reptile is "cold-blooded," that is, its temperature changes with its surroundings. This difference is very important. A dog or wolf can follow its prey for miles without tiring. Most likely, even the advanced mammal-like reptiles could not have done the same. "Cold-blooded" animals also tire more quickly than "warm-blooded" ones.

Left: A much smaller advanced mammal-like reptile called *Oligokyphus*, about twenty inches long. It was found in England.

Right: A small cynodont, *Thrinaxodon,* about eighteen inches long. An adult which may have been a female, was discovered in South Africa. Next to these remains were found the bones of a baby. Could this have been a mother protecting her young?

It would have been most unusual since reptiles do not normally care for their babies. On the other hand, the dog on this page, a full-fledged mammal, takes great care of her puppies and might even fight to the death to protect them from an enemy.

The "sail-backs" and their relatives are the earliest reptiles to show this kind of tooth variety, along with other changes in the skeleton that indicate their ancestral relationship to mammals. Some had good chewing back teeth covered with strong ridges, as in mammals.

A more advanced group of mammal-like reptile meat-eaters were the cynodonts (sign-no-donts), meaning "dog-tooth." These had curved stabbing canines. Also interesting about these cynodonts is the way in which they walked. Reptiles usually drag themselves along the ground on their bellies, inasmuch as their legs protrude at the sides. Reptile derives from a Latin word meaning "to crawl."

Mammals are more upright in their bearing, and have their legs beneath the bulk of their body to hold them off the ground. They are much better at balancing on their feet.

Cynodonts are beginning to show a similar way of walking, as you can see in these pictures. Their bodies are well off the ground.

There were many kinds of advanced mammal-like reptiles during late Permian and Triassic times. We shall see that eventually some of them gave rise to the true mammals by the beginning of the Jurassic period.

"KEY FOSSILS"

At this stage it might be well to mention the significance of certain fossils called "key" fossils. Some are found within specific time limits. This helps scientists date rock layers. Others only appear in the presence of natural resources such as coal, oil, and minerals.

From a scientific point of view, the study of "key" fossils constantly helps us to learn more about the rock strata of the Earth's crust.

TURTLES AND TORTOISES

We now consider one of the most interesting groups of reptiles, the turtles, which came into being about the same time as the dinosaurs, during the Triassic period. Today, they are still going strong. What is more, their life span is among the longest in the animal world. These gentle creatures, especially the land turtles, or tortoises, seem to do everything slowly, and are never in a hurry. Perhaps that may account for their durability on this planet – a stay of up to 200 million years, at least.

Marine turtles live in the sea, tortoises on land, and pond turtles, sometimes called terrapins, live in rivers and marshes.

All of these shelled reptiles have evolved from a common ancestor which has not yet been found. One of the earliest of the group known thus far is *Proganochelys*, depicted at the bottom of the page, which was found in Germany and is about twelve inches long. In many ways it resembles a modern marsh turtle.

The curious thing about turtles is their bony shell, which is like a house built around the body. Scientists theorize that the rib cage slowly evolved into a closed box by growing outside the legs and arms, and as each rib spread out, it joined with its neighbor to form the shell.

Above: One of the living giant tortoises, weighing up to five hundred pounds. They are found in the Galapagos Islands in the Pacific, and the Aldabras Islands in the Indian Ocean. When naturalist Charles Darwin visited the Galapagos (meaning "tortoise") Islands he was impressed with these giants and wrote about them in his book, *The voyage of H.M.S. Beagle.*

The tortoises were hunted mercilessly by sailors when they stopped at the islands for food and water, but today they are protected.

Above: Section of a turtle skeleton, showing the backbone and leg bones inside the shell.

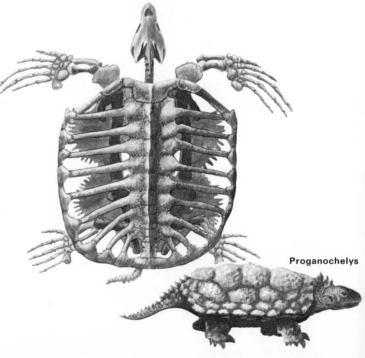

Proganochelys

Right: New Zealand's famous tuatara, a "living fossil." This interesting reptile lays eggs, and of all reptilian eggs, they take the longest time to hatch — about eighteen months. Like its distant cousins, the lizards, the tuatara's tail is very fragile, and can easily break off if it is roughly handled.

THE TUATARA

Throughout the world there are a few plants and animals still living that somehow have survived since very ancient times. The famous coelacanth is, of course, a notable example. Here is another of these "living fossils," *Sphenodon*, found on some of the remote islands off the coast of New Zealand. Tuatara is the local Maori name for it.

This reptile, about eight inches long, looks very much like a lizard, but it really belongs to a different group. It is the only survivor of a reptile branch which reverts to the Triassic period. Paleontologists discern this from the way its skeleton is built. The skull, especially, is not the same as one which identifies a true lizard. The name for this group is Rhyncocephalia, meaning "beak-head."

Another interesting thing about the tuatara is the pineal eye. This is a pinhead-sized structure just below the skin on top of the head. It has many of the makings of a true eye, yet it is hidden. Perhaps it tells the tuatara night from day, even when it is asleep. The pineal eye also exists in some modern lizards and is commonly found in primitive fossil vertebrates.

The tuatara sleeps all night in a burrow made by a petrel, a sea bird. In the morning it comes out to sunbathe, and to catch insects. Meanwhile, the petrel is out at sea looking for fish. It then takes over the burrow and sleeps all day.

The tuatara always lives on islands without any trees. The trees have been killed by thousands of petrels settling on them and poisoning them with their droppings, called guano. Dried guano, however, is an excellent fertilizer and the ground becomes covered by a thick undergrowth of bushes. This attracts a large number of insects and other small creatures, upon which the tuatara feeds.

Opposite: This is the skeleton of a giant sea turtle called *Archelon*. Its shell measured a good twelve feet, and it lived in the seas of the Cretaceous period. Its large, paddle-like feet made it a good swimmer. Today there exists another giant sea turtle, not quite so huge, called the leatherback. Many of our sea turtles today are becoming rare because of over-hunting. Men catch them for their meat to make soup and collect their eggs. It is easy to find their nests, because their tracks reveal their location.

THE SEA REPTILES

Earlier we learned of how successful the reptiles were as conquerors of the land. Some of them even invaded the sea and became water-living vertebrates.

To do this their bodies became adapted for swimming, and many of them took on the shape of fish. Such streamlining helps a water animal to move more easily.

In addition, these sea reptiles had a solid sheath of skin over their fingers and toes, turning them into paddles. They even had fins on their backs and a fish-like tail.

How do we know this? In a fossil skeleton the soft parts are usually missing, such as fins and tail, but sometimes we can tell exactly what these looked like. Some years ago, in a stone quarry at Solnhofen in Germany, some superb specimens of certain marine reptiles were found. Not only was the skeleton preserved, but also the body outline, with the fins and tail actually marked in the stone.

Several kinds of sea reptiles first began to appear during the Triassic period, increasing greatly in numbers during the Jurassic and Cretaceous periods. Then most of them became extinct.

ICHTHYOSAURS

Of all the prehistoric sea reptiles, these were the most fish-like in appearance. Ichthyosaurs (ik-thee-o-sores), meaning "fish lizards," were true reptiles, and as such had to come to the surface occasionally to breathe air, since they had lungs, rather than gills, like fish.

Very fine specimens have been found both in Germany and in England where rocks of the Jurassic period are exposed. A productive area is along part of the Dorset coast in southwestern England. It was here, near the seaside town of Lyme Regis, that the first skeleton of an ichthyosaur was found, and by a little girl. Mary Anning often joined her father in searching for fossils, which he then sold to paleontologists. One morning she spotted the skeleton which is now in the Natural History Museum in London. Even today, visitors might be lucky enough to pick up an ichthyosaur fragment on the beach.

Above: A map showing places where sea reptiles have been found, mostly in England and Germany, but also some in North America.

Left: *Ophthalmosaurus*, an ichthyosaur or fish-reptile which has broad crushing teeth for feeding on shellfish, such as the ammonoid.

Left: A giant *Ichthyosaurus*, which grew up to twenty-four feet in length. Had you ever seen one, you might have mistaken it for a fish because of its shape. There are no gills, however, since this is a reptile that breathes in air through its nostrils. It could not be a porpoise, either, as porpoises are mammals and have horizontal tails.

Another exciting discovery at the Solnhofen quarries has been the skeleton of a mother ichthyosaur with unborn babies still inside her body. This tells scientists that these reptiles gave live birth rather than laying eggs. It would have been useless to lay eggs in the sea, because they would never have hatched. For the fish-shaped ichthyosaur incapable of crawling onto the land, live birth was the only adaptive solution. In their time, the reptile ichthyosaurs were like today's fish-shaped mammals, the whales.

It is very strange the way that sea creatures may be found buried in rocks in what is now solid land. As noted in the first chapter, old seas have been slowly filled in with mud and sediment from rivers and glaciers, so that land now exists where once there was an ocean.

Overleaf: Here is a sea scene of the Jurassic period. Long-necked plesiosaurs are basking on the rocks, while ichthyosaurs are leaping like dolphins in the sea.

37

Right: Marine life flourished in the Cretaceous seas. Well-preserved fossils of sea-living vertebrates have been found in the chalk deposits of Kansas. At one time this part of America was partly submerged by an inland sea.

PLESIOSAURS

This word means "more like a lizard". These sea reptiles, abundant during the Jurassic and Cretaceous periods, shared the seas with the ichthyosaurs and marine turtles.

Somebody once described a plesiosaur as "a turtle with a snake pushed through it" – an excellent description for this animal.

Whereas ichthyosaurs never ventured on land, it is quite possible that these plesiosaurs could do so. Like seals, they might have hauled themselves onto the beach or the rocks to rest. Maybe this is where they laid their eggs, like turtles, but scientists really do not know, as they have never found a clutch of them.

Plesiosaurs "rowed" themselves along with their strong paddle-like limbs. Their body structure suggests that they could even swim backward, something like the way a man can change direction in a canoe. He simply uses the paddles in a reverse motion.

The plesiosaur's long, twisting neck must have been useful for darting after fish, since these reptiles were not very fast swimmers. And a fish would not have had much chance of escaping from those sharp teeth.

Some plesiosaurs grew to an enormous 12 yards long. Plesiosaurs hunted fish along with creatures such as ammonoids, squid-like animals with a shell and tentacles. Ammonoids came in all sizes, from that of a small button to two yards across.

Above: This long-necked plesiosaur, which could be up to forty-two feet long, is pursuing a fish. Although it moves slowly, its neck is built for twisting and turning very quickly – just right for fishing!

Right: *Elasmosaurus*, one of the largest plesiosaurs. It was found in North America.

Here again, in 1823, it was young Mary Anning of Lyme Regis who found the first plesiosaur.

The scene above of a Cretaceous sea contains many sea reptiles. Shown on the far left is a plesiosaur near the surface. Below it is a marine lizard, called a mosasaur. On the right is a diving bird, next to a larger-headed plesiosaur called *Kronosaurus*. Gliding overhead is the giant pterosaur, *Pteranodon*.

Sometimes strange stories are circulated of water creatures that might be survivors from this ancient world of sea creatures. In fact, paleontologists once called them sea dragons.

One well-publicized legend of such a living creature today is Scotland's "Loch Ness monster." It may only be a legend, but the plesiosaurs were certainly real. It is still possible for people to find parts of their skeletons. Where there are cliffs of Jurassic or Cretaceous rocks along the coast of England and Australia, as well as places in the United States, (especially Kansas, at one time partly submerged by an inland sea), teeth or parts of backbone may be found.

Above: This form of sea reptile, called *Kronosaurus*, belongs with the short-necked group of plesiosaurs. It had a short neck with a huge head, nine feet long, and must have hunted other sea reptiles, as well as large shellfish.

THE RULING REPTILES – ARCHOSAURS

This is the name that has been given to a group of early reptiles which began to appear during the Triassic period. Their direct descendants, also called archosaurs, include the dinosaurs, the crocodiles, the pterosaurs, and also the birds.

This is concluded from the way in which their bones and skulls are built. Remember, bones are important to a paleontologist, as he has little else to study when he finds a fossil. An entomologist displays his insect collection according to the variation of their wings, and in a similar way, a paleontologist looks at bones and teeth of his fossils.

Some of the reptiles in these pictures look like crocodiles, and at one time paleontologists thought they were the ancestors of our modern crocodiles. This is not so, because there are some important differences in their skeletons.

If you look closely at *Rutiodon*, you will see that the nostrils are at the back of its snout, close to the eyes. In true crocodiles they are at the far end. This slight difference is one way of telling them apart.

Above: The larger reptile, twenty feet long, is *Rutiodon,* a crocodile-like thecodont called a phytosaur. Above it is *Stagonolepis*, from Kansas, some ten feet long, and a different kind of four-legged thecodont.

Right: *Shansisuchus,* up to thirteen feet long. *Shansisuchus* and *Chasmatosaurus* are both early archosaurs, called thecodonts, living during the Triassic period. The thecodonts include the two-legged ancestors of dinosaurs, true crocodiles, pterosaurs, and birds.

These crocodile-like creatures are called phytosaurs. Together with the early archosaurs, they are known as thecodonts. This group became extinct by the end of the Triassic period.

CROCODILES

By the end of the Triassic period the true crocodile came into existence. They became a flourishing group and we still have some with us today. We might even call them "living archosaurs," since their family tree goes right back to these early reptiles. In fact, crocodiles are the nearest living cousins to dinosaurs.

Much of the study of early Triassic crocodiles has been done by the American Museum of Natural

Above: The picture is that of a reptile called *Chasmatosaurus*, about four feet long. It had a peculiar down-turned snout and many sharp teeth for catching slippery fish.

Right: *Protosuchus*, one of the first true crocodiles, only three feet long. It was found in Arizona and its body structure was similar to today's crocodiles.

Along with most early archosaurs, it had hard, bony plates buried in the skin. These are still found in modern crocodiles, especially along their backs. That is why only the skin on the underside is used for making crocodile leather shoes and handbags.

History in New York. Some fine specimens of *Protosuchus* were found in Arizona, while other remains of early crocodiles have been found in South Africa.

MODERN CROCODILES

Although many ancient crocodiles lived in the sea, there is only one species today which lives in salt water near the coasts. This is the salt-water crocodile occurring from India to the Philippines and northern Australia. A record size some years ago was 25 feet. This crocodile will attack man.

Normally crocodiles are shy of humans and slip into the water when they are disturbed. This is when they could be dangerous to bathers.

Modern crocodiles and alligators, both descendants of ancient Jurassic crocodiles, are only found in warmer parts of the world. There is one obvious difference between true crocodiles and alligators. In a true crocodile there is a notch behind the tip of the snout, on both sides of the jaw. When the mouth closes, a large tooth on either side of the lower

jaw fits into these notches so that the two teeth are exposed. In an alligator these teeth are hidden in special sockets.

LIZARDS AND SNAKES

Among reptiles living today, lizards and snakes are the most numerous. They are descended from ancestors that lived during the Permian period, some 250 million years ago.

There are approximately 2,500 living lizards, and the same number of snakes, grouped together under the classification *Squamata*, meaning "scaly."

Although snakes are legless, and lizards generally have limbs, this is not always so. The slowworms

Left: A real crocodile giant called *Deinosuchus*, lived in the Cretaceous seas and grew to fifty feet in length. There is nothing like it today, as a large-sized modern crocodile would be about fifteen feet long.

and many of the skinks are lizards with very small reduced limbs. Some have none at all. Some snakes, notably the pythons and boas, have tiny traces of hind limb girdles beneath the skin near their tails.

Two more obvious differences between lizards and snakes are the eyes and jaws. Lizards have movable eyelids, but snakes have none – they are constantly staring. Also, most lizards have solid jaws that only move up and down from the hinges at the back. Snake jaws, on the other hand, consist of loosely jointed bones that permit sideways expansion as well. Snakes, therefore, can take in meals wider than their heads, swallowing seemingly impossible prey.

True lizards existed by Triassic times, some of them already very specialized in form. These were gliding lizards whose extraordinarily lengthened ribs supported membranes for gliding from branch to branch.

Snakes are lizard descendants and by the Cretaceous period constrictor snakes, like our own pythons, up to twenty yards long, were living in Africa. Poisonous snakes developed later.

Some of the largest lizards, however, lived in the seas of the Cretaceous period at the time of dinosaurs. Called Mosasaurs, they grew up to twenty-one feet long. With their powerful teeth and strong paddle-like limbs they must have been a peril to every other sea reptile and fish they encountered. Mosasaurs are an early offshoot from ancestral monitor lizards.

Above: This strange creature is the horned chameleon of Africa, looking like a miniature dinosaur. It is a lizard and completely harmless. Chameleons can move their eyes separately in all directions, catch food on their flip-out tongues, and change color.

MODERN SNAKES AND LIZARDS

Judging by their numbers and variety, these are certainly the most adaptable reptiles today. In spite of no legs, snakes can move about quite well. Some crawl or climb, others swim or burrow, and some even "fly." By flattening its body, a flying snake is able to leap into the air and glide from one tree branch to another.

A snake is extremely sensitive to vibrations, and can feel footsteps along the ground then slip away long before it might otherwise be seen. Even so, people fear snakes and say they will attack. This rarely happens, unless you pick one up, tread on it, or tease it. A snake's bite is only poisonous if the snake carries poison that is injected through special teeth. There are some snakes whose poison can be fatal, and these should either be avoided or handled with extreme care.

Below: This is a mosasaur, a giant marine lizard found in Holland near the river Meuse. Thus its name – the "Meuse lizard."

Below: Two examples of odd prehistoric lizards. The one above is *Keuhneosaurus*, which had long skin-covered ribs, that looked like wings. It could glide through the air. Today a similar-looking lizard lives in the jungles of the Far East, and is called the flying dragon. Below it is a long-necked *Tanystropheus*, measuring a total length of twelve feet. Perhaps the long neck was used as a kind of fishing rod that was stretched into the water to catch food as the animal stood on the water's edge.

Lizards can also crawl, climb, swim, burrow and "fly." They are far less dangerous, since only two are poisonous – the desert-living Mexican beaded lizard, and the Arizona gila monster. Both are fat, sluggish and brightly colored. It takes these reptiles a long time to inject their poison as they have no special poison fangs.

DINOSAURS

Of all the prehistoric animals ever found the dinosaurs must surely be among the most fascinating and best-known. Among their number were some of the largest and strangest animals that have ever lived.

The word *Dinosauria* (die-no-sore-ee-a) means "mighty or terrible lizards," and was given to this group by Sir Richard Owen, the first director of the Natural History Museum in London, early in the last century.

It was about that time that the first remains were being discovered, including some enormous bones. Since then dinosaurs of all shapes and sizes have been found all over the world.

Did the dinosaurs really deserve their name, and were they all monsters as terrible as they appeared? Well, we shall see.

The "dinosaur family tree" is shown on the opposite page. Dinosaurs were first found in the Triassic period. By then they had already branched off into two groups. One is the ornithischia (or-nee-this-kee-a) which means "bird hipped," shown on the left. The saurischia (sore-is-kee-a), meaning "reptile-hipped" is shown on the right.

Above: This is the hip girdle of a saurischian or "lizard-hipped" dinosaur. The two lower bones, the *ischium* and *pubis,* are placed wide apart.

Below: The hip girdle of an ornithischian or "bird-hipped" dinosaur. Here the ischium and pubis lie close together. Such a hip girdle is similar to that found in birds. The first such hip bones found, in fact, were thought to belong to giant birds.

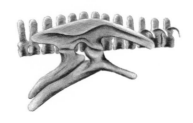

Both these orders of dinosaurs continued through the Jurassic into the Cretaceous period. Then they mysteriously died out, and nobody knows why.

We can only guess at what went wrong. Perhaps they became too big and clumsy, and could no longer compete with other animals. One big handicap must have been their tiny brains. Even in the largest dinosaur this was no bigger than a fist.

Left: The two-legged thecodont ancestors of dinosaurs were quite small. This is *Euparkeria*, no bigger than a barn yard goose. It lived during the early Triassic period, and its place is at the bottom of the dinosaur family tree on the opposite page. Imagine a slender goose with scales instead of feathers, arms for wings, and a beak full of teeth. This gives us some idea of what these dinosaur ancestors might have looked like. They were all tiny, and ran about on their hind legs. The body was held low, and the tail was used to act as a balance.

The earliest dinosaurs were two-legged like their ancestors. Much later, as many dinosaurs became larger, their heavy bodies forced them to come down on all fours, especially if they were plant-eaters. The hunters, both large and small, remained on their hind legs, so that they could move more quickly and run down their prey.

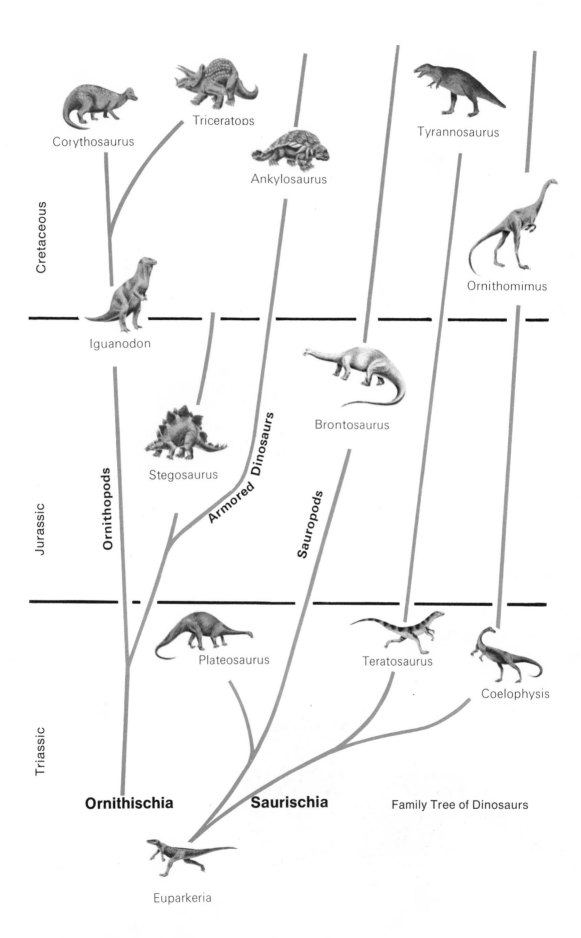

Corythosaurus

Triceratops

Ankylosaurus

Tyrannosaurus

Ornithomimus

Cretaceous

Iguanodon

Brontosaurus

Armored Dinosaurs

Stegosaurus

Ornithopods

Jurassic

Sauropods

Plateosaurus

Teratosaurus

Coelophysis

Triassic

Ornithischia

Saurischia

Family Tree of Dinosaurs

Euparkeria

Another possibility is that they died from a kind of starvation. Most of them were plant-eaters, and during the Cretaceous period a significant change took place. Up till then the plant-eaters had lived in a world of evergreen plants that kept their leaves through the year.

Now new kinds of trees began to appear, similar to those growing today, which shed their leaves in autumn. A shortage of food might have resulted, so that there was not enough to go round. Once the plant-eaters died out, the hunting dinosaurs would have gone as well.

THE PLANT-EATERS

Some of these magnificent giants grew to never-to-be-repeated sizes, mostly made up of neck and tail.

Below: This is *Diplodocus* (Dip-lod-o-kus). It means a "double beam" and refers to its shape. The long neck and tail are like two beams at each end of the body. A lot has been learned about these skeletons and the way the bones fit together. They are like machines full of joints and levers.

Left: This giant with its neck in the air is *Brachiosaurus* (bray-kee-o-sore-us). It has been found in Africa and North America, and belongs to the Jurassic period. Unlike the other giant plant-eating dinosaurs, its front legs were very much longer than its hind ones. With its neck held straight in the air it would have been forty feet tall. This is one of the heaviest four-legged animals ever to exist on earth, and weighed up to eighty-five tons.

Below left: *Plateosaurus*, of Triassic age and from South Africa, was much smaller, only about twenty-one feet long. Looking like a small *Diplodocus*, it is one of the earlier kinds of plant-eating "lizard-hipped" dinosaurs.

The largest so far known was *Diplodocus*, which was found in Wyoming. It measured 98 feet from snout to tail end.

Many of these giants' footprints have been found where they had once walked through the mud. Someone once asked why it was that no evidence of the tail could be found where it might have dragged along the ground. The answer was that the dinosaur was probably walking along the bottom of a lake, so that the tail was floating!

What were these giants doing in the water? The answer is that they were far too heavy to move about easily on land. Some of them weighed up to thirty tons!

The relatively tiny head is actually the most interesting part to study. The eye sockets and nose opening on top of the head is common to water animals such as frogs or crocodiles.

The teeth also tell us something. They are at the front of the jaws, and resemble a row of pegs. Stretching out its long neck, a giant like *Brontosaurus* would use its teeth like a gardener's rake, drawing in the soft vegetation growing along the water's edge.

THE HUNTING DINOSAURS

Whereas *Brontosaurus* and its cousins were harmless plant-eating giants, there were other dinosaurs during the Age of Reptiles that hunted their prey and fed on meat. This conclusion is drawn from their sharp, curved teeth and strong claws.

These flesh-eaters ran about on their hind legs, and must have been very active. They were quite small at first – some were no bigger than chickens.

You may have noticed that all of the two-legged dinosaurs, whether hunters or plant-eaters, had long tails, which helped balance them when they ran about. Their bodies would have been top-heavy without a long tail.

As we follow the progression of dinosaurs it is interesting to note how the hunters kept pace with the plant-eaters. As the ancient vegetarians increased in size, so did the flesh-eaters.

The most awesome of these flesh-eaters finally appeared in the Cretaceous period, toward the end of the Age of Reptiles.

Above: Although most reptile hunters have sharp teeth for catching their prey, there have been some without teeth. This one is called *Ornithomimus* (or-nee-the-my-mus) and was about twelve feet long. It could only catch and eat small animals because it had a toothless beak like an ostrich. It probably fed mostly on fruit and soft plants, and stole birds' eggs. *Ornithomimus* means "bird mimic," so named for its bird-like beak.

Overleaf: This is a swamp of the Upper Jurassic period in Colorado. The water is supporting *Brachiosaurus's* tremendous weight. Another giant, *Brontosaurus* is lurking on the shore.

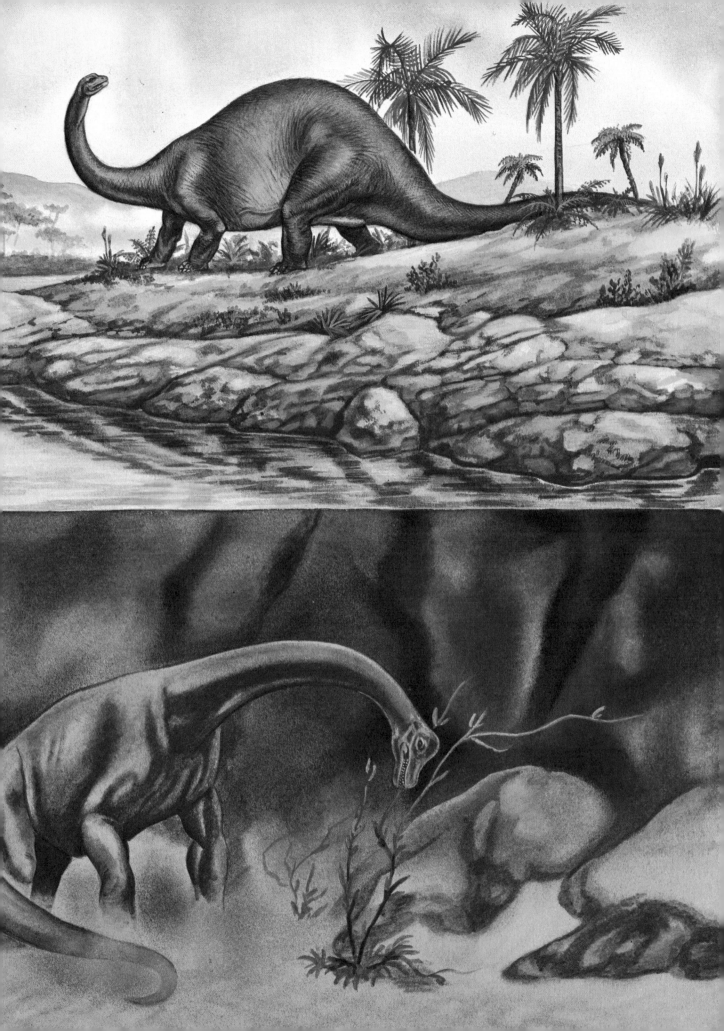

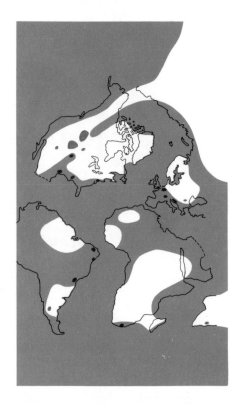

THE TYRANT KING

We are now about to learn of one of the most famous of all the dinosaurs that ever existed. Most people have heard about this monster. It is that fearsome hunter, *Tyrannosaurus rex* (tie-ran-o-sore-us rex). Its name means "king of the tyrant lizards."

When it was first discovered, paleontologists must have been astonished at its size. This amazing reptile was about fifty feet long, and stood nearly twenty-five feet tall. It had powerful hind legs, each with three toes and large claws. Its head was four feet long, and contained a battery of sharp, curved teeth with saw-like edges.

Tyrannosaurus rex had tiny arms. They ended in two small fingers that seem to have been quite useless, as they could not even reach its mouth!

Tyrannosaurus must have run its prey down on its powerful hind legs and attacked only with its ferocious and powerful head.

Above: This map shows the places in which dinosaurs from the Cretaceous period have been discovered. All of the blue area was sea. This is about the time when the Atlantic Ocean is thought to have formed as North America and Europe slowly drifted apart. Since dinosaurs on both these continents were similar, there must have been a land bridge somewhere.

Right: *Tyrannosaurus rex*, the Tyrant King who preyed on the other reptiles during the Cretaceous period. Probably no other animal has ever existed quite like this. He certainly deserves his name.

All the meat-eaters including *Tyrannosaurus*, as well as the large plant-eaters like *Brontosaurus*, were "lizard-hipped" or saurischia.

The Age of Dinosaurs is ending. In the next, the Tertiary period, there will be none left.

IGUANODON

Pictured on the left of this page is a rather famous dinosaur, *Iguanodon* (ig-gwah-no-don), which means "iguana tooth." Apart from some odd footprints, it was the first of the dinosaurs ever to be discovered.

It all started with a tooth found by the roadside near the town of Horsham in Sussex, England.

One day in 1823, Mrs Mantell, the wife of a doctor, picked it up and showed it to her husband. Dr Mantell was a paleontologist as well as a doctor, and he became very interested in it. Later, some more teeth and a bone or two were found in a nearby quarry.

From these few fragments, Dr Mantell tried to create a drawing of this creature. One curious find puzzled him: it was cone-shaped, rounded at one end, and tapering to a point. The doctor concluded that it might be a horn. He placed it on the nose of the animal on his drawing, and he also drew the animal on all fours.

From many more remains since found it is now known that *Iguanodon* moved about upright on two hind legs, and that the "horn" was actually a spiky thumb on the creature's hand.

Because of this thumb, this reptile is sometimes called "the Dagger-thumb." The thumb might have been used for defense against enemies, or perhaps for tearing down branches of trees so that it could feed on the leaves.

Dr Mantell named it after some present-day New World lizards called iguanas, because their teeth look similar to the tooth his wife found.

Modern iguanas and the dinosaur *Iguanodon* are both vegetarians. Otherwise there is no connection since dinosaurs had died out completely and could have nothing to do with any living lizard.

Iguanodon lived during the Cretaceous period. It was one of the "bird-hips" and its remains and footprints have been found in parts of England and Europe. In Belgium a herd of twenty were found in a coal mine, buried together. No one knows what disaster overtook them. They might have fallen over a cliff to their death, or been trapped in a swamp.

You can see this fine collection of *iguanodons* in the Natural History Museum in Brussels, Belgium.

Above: *Iguanodon,* the first dinosaur ever to be discovered. Notice the spiky thumbs, which Dr Mantell mistook for a horn on the nose before the skeleton was reconstructed.

Right: Here is *Pachycephalosaurus*, the giant bone-headed lizard. This dinosaur's skull was twenty inches long, the bone was ten inches thick, and yet its brain was no larger than a walnut.

Right: One of the duckbilled dinosaurs called *Corythosaurus*. It had webs between its toes for swimming. It fed on water plants and perhaps shell fish, and could also dive into water to escape enemies.

   The helmet on its head was hollow and may have contained air so that the duckbill could breathe when it went under water.

Below: Three examples of the hollow spaces in the nose region or on top of the head of duckbills. The pink portion is solid bone, and the space inside is where air might have been stored.

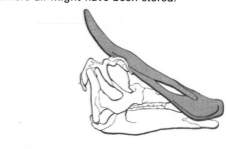

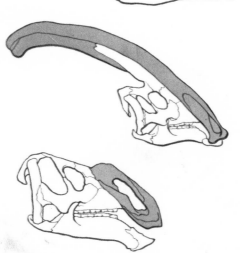

DUCKBILLS

There are several kinds of "bird-hipped" dinosaurs that lived close to the water and even went in occasionally. They are called duckbills because of their flat duck-like mouths which they used for feeding on water plants. The mouth was lined with rows of teeth, and as many as 2,400 teeth have been counted in one kind of duckbill alone.

We also know that these reptiles had tails which were flattened sideways, which tells us that they were able to wade and even swim in the water. Thus they could reach water plants, and also escape from enemies such as *Tyrannosaurus rex*.

Some of the duckbills had curious bony growths on their heads, looking like helmets or long horns. These were hollow. Nobody really knows what good these "helmets" were, although there are many theories. Can you think of any?

ARMORED DINOSAURS

Whereas *Iguanodon* could have run away to escape an enemy, and the duckbills could have dived into the water, there were other "bird-hipped" dinosaurs far too heavy and clumsy to move away fast enough.

Some were covered in a kind of armor consisting of thick, bony shields and spikes that served for protection. One of these was the Jurassic *Stegosaurus* (steg-o-sore-us), meaning "plate lizard." It had a tiny head on a large body. One peculiarity was the two rows of bony plates along its back. They were not even joined to the backbone, and we can only speculate on what their purpose was. Perhaps it was for protection, like the spiky tail. This could have been lashed side to side, to drive away an enemy.

In spite of its huge size, up to twenty feet long, *Stegosaurus* had a tiny brain and must have been very dull indeed.

Ankylosaurus of the Cretaceous period was another kind of armored dinosaur covered with bony plates. All down the sides of its body were large, protective spines. The tail ended in a bony lump, looking something like a club.

A "SECOND BRAIN"

Perhaps you have heard at some time vague references by people talking about a dinosaur having an extra brain somewhere near its tail. (Some of the creatures might well have done with an extra one.) On the opposite page is pictured the head of *Pachycephalosaurus* (pack-ee-sef-a-low-sore-us), which means "thick-headed lizard."

The "second brain" that people talk about is really a swelling of the spinal cord which runs through the backbone to the tail. An animal does things in a deliberate fashion with its brain. Humans think logically with theirs. However, this secondary swelling acts as a kind of automatic signal box, and produces a reflex. In the dinosaurs, this reflex nerve center controlled the back legs.

HORNED DINOSAURS

Animals have developed yet another way of protecting themselves – with horns. Deer, antelope, cattle, goats and sheep will use their horns to fight during the mating season, or to defend themselves from predators such as lions and wolves. They will even defend their young. An African antelope has been known to challenge a lion when protecting its calf, and even drive the lion away.

Triceratops (try-ser-a-tops) was a well-known horned dinosaur found in North America. The horned dinosaurs were another group of "bird-hips." *Triceratops* means "three-horn face." It grew to twenty-one feet in length, a clumsy giant with a horn on its snout and a larger one above each eye. Although the body had no armor, there was a large bony frill standing up over its neck. This would have given *Triceratops* good protection, as long as he faced his enemy.

One can imagine the terrible battles that must have taken place when *Tyrannosaurus rex* arrived on the scene. The giant hunter would have leaped forward to attack, and *Triceratops* would have turned to meet him with head down. The outcome would then hinge upon which ever animal moved the fastest. *Tyrannosaurus* would try to leap over or around those dangerous horns, land on the back of *Triceratops* and use his razor-like teeth. This attack might not always be effective, assuming for example, that *Triceratops* got in a blow first with his sharp horns. Either of these antagonists might have killed the other.

Fossil bones of hunter and hunted have been found mixed together, as if the two opponents had both died in a death struggle.

Above: A nest of dinosaur eggs. This exciting discovery was made during the 1920s by an expedition from the American Museum of Natural History in New York. The team went into the Gobi Desert in Mongolia where many fossils were found. One day some sandstone rocks were being examined, and the eggs were found lying in a neat pile, just as they had been laid over 70 million years ago. They were from six to eight inches long, as hard as stone, and with cracked shells. These eggs were so well preserved that it was possible to examine the contents and discern what some of the bones of the unborn young looked like.

Remains of what could have been one of the parents showed that these eggs came from a small dinosaur, about seven feet long when full-grown, called *Protoceratops*. This means the "early horn-face," and it lived long before *Triceratops*. It also had a shield over its neck, but only a small knob on its nose instead of any horns. So many fossils of *Protoceratops* were found that every growth stage, from hatching young to adult, could be reconstructed.

Left: Here is *Triceratops,* the "three-horn face" dinosaur.

FLYING REPTILES

Long ago, insects became the first flying creatures. The first success among the vertebrates was during the Age of Reptiles.

In the Age of Reptiles, during the Triassic period, some small reptiles gave rise to the pterosaurs (ter-o-sores), meaning "wing lizards." This occurred in a remarkable way. The arms of their small, tree-climbing ancestors slowly evolved into wings.

Upon examining the wing bones, paleontologists discovered a curiosity. Half the length of a wing was composed of the normal arm bones; the rest was a long wrist bone and a single, extra long finger. Three other fingers projected as short hooks halfway along the wing, across which was stretched a leathery skin from the ankle to the tip of the long finger.

This is why some of these reptiles are called pterodactyls (tero-dak-tils). Pterodactyl means "wing-finger." How such a wing would work in flight is a mystery. It does not appear to be strong enough. One answer could be that pterosaurs merely glided through the air with their wings held out stiffly, as seagulls do.

For this kind of gliding, pterosaurs would need an air current into which to launch themselves. They may have lived in flocks on cliffs near the sea, or in mountains where breezes prevail.

To fly, they would need only to spring into the air, open their wings and glide away. When at rest, the three small clawed fingers and the clawed toes could be used for clinging onto cliff ledges or trees in the manner of bats.

Because many skeletons were buried in soft mud under the sea, which turned into fine limestone, some interesting details have been found. Wing bones were hollow, making them lightweight and strong as in birds. Skulls have been so well preserved that it has been possible to get some idea of the shape and size of the brain.

What did pterosaurs feed on? They may have caught their prey in the air, if they were fast enough. The most likely answer is that many of them flew over the water and scooped up fish near the surface, as some sea birds do today.

Below: Flying over the tree is the greatest of the pterosaurs, called *Pteranodon.* It had a large toothless beak, and a bony crest behind the head. The wings were about twenty-five feet across.

Below this is *Pterodactylus*, some specimens of which were only sparrow-sized. It had front teeth that pointed forward like long spikes.

At the bottom is *Dsungaripterus*, looking very much like a bat.

ANCIENT BIRDS

Our knowledge of what birds were like in prehistoric times is sparse. Few remains have been found because bird bones do not fossilize easily.

There is one bird, however, which has taught us a great deal about the origin of feathered vertebrates and how they evolved from reptiles. It is called *Archaeopteryx* (ar-kee-op-tur-icks), meaning the "ancient wing."

Left: *Archaeopteryx*, the "halfway" bird. Three good skeletons have been found of this earliest feathered vertebrate. Two are in Germany and the other is in the Natural History Museum in London. Although the head of the London specimen is missing, a perfect impression of the braincase has recently been found. *Archaeopteryx* was a poor flyer with little strength in its wings, because its chest muscles, unlike those of modern birds, were small. Gliding from tree to tree, it used its tail for balance.

Below: Two primitive toothed birds from the Cretaceous period. *Ichthyornis,* the size of a tern, and the diving bird *Hesperornis* (bottom).

ARCHAEOPTERYX

About the middle of the nineteenth century the imprint of feathers was found in a limestone quarry in Solnhofen, Germany, where the sea reptiles were discovered. The limestone rocks in the quarry belonged to the Age of Reptiles, within the Jurassic period. What was a bird doing among the pterosaurs and dinosaurs?

When a complete skeleton was found, what a sensation it caused! Here was a reptile's skeleton, yet it was the size of a crow and covered in feathers.

The feathers were like those of a modern bird, fixed to the wings, tail and body, and it could have looked like a normal bird.

There were, nevertheless, three peculiar features.

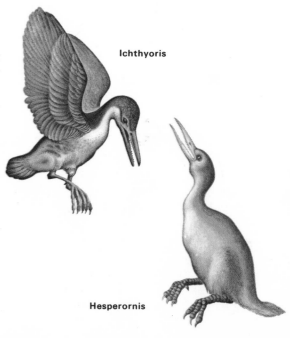

Ichthyoris

Hesperornis

Firstly, *Archaeopteryx* had teeth in its jaws. Secondly, three short fingers with claws stood out halfway along each wing. Thirdly, it had a long tail trailing behind, with feathers in pairs down both sides. By contrast, a modern bird's tail bone is very short, and the feathers are spread out like a fan. *Archaeopteryx*, then, is a lizard that looks like a bird.

SEA BIRDS

Long after *Archaeopteryx* had come and gone, a number of more modern-looking birds appeared. There are examples of sea birds from the Cretaceous period, well preserved in the soft chalk rocks of Kansas.

Pictured on the opposite page is *Ichthyornis*. Below it is *Hesperornis*, a powerful swimmer without wings. Even so, it could catch fish in its toothed beak.

GIANT BIRDS

Ostriches and emus are modern running birds. Their ancestors were larger and some were fierce hunters.

The giant moas of New Zealand could grow to 3 feet tall. They are thought to have lived during the Stone Age when man first came to New Zealand. Their descendants, the Maoris, tell tales of how their ancestors used to hunt these birds.

Above: One of the giant moas found in New Zealand. The first remains turned up when a farmer found a pile of bones when he was burying a dead horse. A bone was shown to Richard Owen of the Natural History Museum in London and he said it came from a giant bird. He proved to be right.

Far left: *Diatryma*, a giant flightless bird that probably hunted the small ancestors of modern mammals.

Left: *Phororhachos*, another hunter, with a vulture-like beak.

THE DAWN PERIOD

The extinction of the dinosaurs still remains a mystery. Together with the pterosaurs and sea reptiles, they had all disappeared by the end of the Cretaceous period. A new stage was beginning – the Age of Mammals. It started about sixty-five million years ago.

The Paleocene epoch marks the beginning of the Tertiary period which followed the Cretaceous period. The Paleocene and later the Eocene epochs marked the beginning of the kind of animals that we see around us today. We keep mammals in our zoos, on our farms, and as pets. Humans, too, are mammals.

We and our mammalian cousins have many advantages over the old reptiles. Our bodies are always warm so that we can keep active during both winter and summer periods, and we can also live in cold surroundings where reptiles cannot exist. Should we feel cold, we can warm up by wearing thicker clothing, or by "shivering" our muscles – something that reptiles cannot do.

Below left: This is *Morganucodon*, one of the earliest mammals so far discovered. It is only about five inches long, not very much larger than a shrew. It lived alongside the dinosaurs, as far back as the late Triassic period, and was found in Britain. It was a restless hunter of insects which it caught in its sharp teeth.

Morganucodon although a true mammal, was not directly related to the modern mammals of today's world. It may have appeared shrew-like, but living shrews belong to an entirely different group. Shrews are insectivores, a group of mammals that once included the direct ancestors of all the modern mammals with the exception of the pouched and egg-laying mammals.

Another difference is that mammals have babies which they protect and feed on milk. "Mammal" comes from the Latin word for a breast. Also, mammals have better brains.

Just like the reptiles, the mammals started in an unobtrusive way. Some even existed when there were living dinosaurs about. They were tiny opossum-like creatures, only a few inches long, living in the undergrowth of the Jurassic and Cretaceous jungles, right under the noses of the dinosaurs.

Left: Here is a tiny, ancient, chisel-toothed mammal called *Ctenacodon*.

THE PLATYPUS

When the first British settlers arrived in Australia, they found an unusual animal which had the overall form of a mole, yet had a bill like that of a duck, swimming feet, and a paddle-shaped tail. It laid eggs, yet it was furry. Then a surprising thing happened. The babies that hatched from these eggs fed on their mother's milk!

Nobody knew what to make of this, because it was the first time a mammal had been found that laid eggs. We now know why. The platypus is a "living fossil," a link between reptiles and mammals which has somehow managed to survive to this day.

It is believed that the first mammals all laid eggs and that they evolved from reptiles. Today, there are only two kinds of these animals left, the platypus and the echidna, an Australian spiny anteater.

With its odd-shaped beak, the platypus swims along the bottom of a stream or lake sifting food from the mud in the same manner as a duck. It feeds on water animals like crayfish. On land it digs up worms to eat.

Below: Here is a platypus in its burrow. Inside its tunnel, the platypus builds a nest of grass and leaves and here it lays its two eggs. When the babies hatch out and the mother has to leave them to search for food, she blocks up the entrance to protect the little ones from enemies that might enter the burrow.

Right: The platypus has rarely been bred in captivity. However, there is one success story of an Australian naturalist who kept a pair in a swimming pool with tunnels leading off to nest boxes. The female laid eggs, and one of the babies grew up into a healthy youngster.

Many animals have poisonous weapons to protect themselves or to kill their prey. The platypus is the only mammal to have this weapon. It is a pair of poison spurs found on the heels of the male.

THE ECHIDNA

This is the other egg-laying mammal that has managed to survive side by side with the platypus since ancient times. It also lives in Australia, but unlike the platypus, is found in New Guinea as well.

Another name for it is the spiny anteater, which it gets because of its covering of sharp spines similar to those of a porcupine, and its habit of eating termites or white ants. With its powerful feet and claws, it will dig into a termite hill for food. It has a long snout with a tiny mouth at the end. As the termites come crawling into the open, it darts out its sticky tongue to catch them.

Although the echidna lays eggs, it does not make a nest. Instead, it puts the eggs into a pouch underneath its body and carries them around wherever it goes.

MARSUPIALS

This word comes from the Latin for pouch. In Australia there are many kinds of marsupial that carry their babies in pockets, or pouches, such as the kangaroo, the wombat, the Tasmanian "wolf," and the Koala, or teddy bear.

Why is it that they are all living in Australia? What is thought to have happened is this. As modern mammals increased, they gradually took the place of the egg-layers and marsupials in most parts of the world. But many of the more primitive mammals managed to move into Australia when it was still joined to Asia. Then, a long while ago, the sea broke through, and Australia became a huge island. At last the marsupials were safe from their competition, and could go on living undisturbed. They have been doing so ever since.

Left: The echidna, like the platypus, is a true "living fossil" — a relic from the days long ago when all mammals laid eggs. This one is found in Australia and New Guinea. There is another one, called the long-beaked echidna, only found in New Guinea. It has a particularly long snout, but not so many spines. As with porcupines, the spines are very soft in the baby stage, but harden later on. Otherwise, it would be a rather prickly bundle for the mother to carry in her pouch.

Though the platypus does not do very well in captivity, a number of echidnas have been kept in zoos for many years. In the London zoo one echidna lived for nearly thirty years. Some platypuses were kept for a while in the Bronx zoo in New York City, but were a disappointment to visitors because they were so shy. Every time an airplane flew over, they dived for cover.

Above: This is the lovable koala, resembling a teddy bear, which still lives wild in parts of Australia, mostly in protected parks where visitors can observe them. This marsupial was named after the United States president, Theodore Roosevelt, called Teddy by his friends. Koalas were once hunted for their fur, and in one year millions of skins were collected. Koala is aboriginal for "I do not drink". The animals seem to get all the moisture they need from eating eucalyptus leaves.

Right: *Thylacosmilus*, about six feet long, was a large marsupial with huge canine teeth. It looked very much like the great saber-toothed cats which hunted throughout North America long ago. On the far right is *Borhyaena*, a marsupial meat-eater about four feet long, looking somewhat like a mountain lion. Both of them have been found in South America.

These prehistoric meat-eating pouched mammals were once a very successful group in South America. For as long as South America remained a separate continent from North America these marsupials were the only hunters. At that time, the true dogs, cats and weasels lived only in North America, Eurasia and Africa.

FOSSIL MARSUPIALS

At one time these primitive mammals lived throughout the world, and many have been found in north and south America and in Europe.

The earliest marsupials lived in the Cretaceous period, right alongside the dinosaurs, and looked very much as the North American opossum does today. They probably lived in trees in the same way, and hunted a variety of small animals.

Slowly the marsupials evolved into all kinds of animals, big and small, plant-eaters as well as meat-eaters, just like placental mammals. The placental mammals include most of the modern mammals, like dogs and sheep. When placental young are born they are much more developed than marsupial young, and need not spend any time in a pouch.

Right: Although most marsupials live in Australia, there are some in North and South America. The best known is the Virginia opossum, a tree-climber that eats just about everything. It has a tail with which it can cling to branches. Sometimes an opossum will lie quite still when it is frightened, as if it had died, which is how the expression "playing possum" came about.

THE AGE OF MAMMALS

As we have already seen, both marsupial and placental mammals were beginning to appear toward the end of the Age of Reptiles. The placentals started as tiny, shrew-like animals and they were the ancestors of all the mammals other than marsupials and egg-layers.

Gradually the placental mammals developed into all shapes and sizes. By the time of the Eocene epoch (the second division of the Tertiary period), there were many small mammals in evidence. We can recognize them as the direct ancestors of the modern mammals.

By examining various fossils of mammals from the Eocene epoch up to the present day, it has been possible to trace the evolution of different branches of modern mammals, such as horses, elephants, cats, rabbits, and even of ourselves.

Below top: *Uintatherium*, one of the giant plant-eaters, up to twelve feet long. It had powerful grinding teeth and a number of bony horns on its head. It lived only during the early part of the Age of Mammals.

Center: *Coryphon* was about eight feet long. It was found by some fishermen on the seabed when they discovered a piece of jawbone in their net just off the coast of England. Many complete specimens have since been found in North America.

Bottom: *Phenacodus* looked like the earliest ancestors of modern hoofed mammals. It was a plant-eater about three feet long, found in Wyoming.

It has the full number of hoof-tipped toes — five on each foot. This little mammal lived at the same time as the tiny horse, *Eohippus*. Some time before, mammals just like *Phenacodus* are thought to have given rise to the first horses. This shows that sometimes a fairly unchanged ancestor can continue to live alongside its descendants.

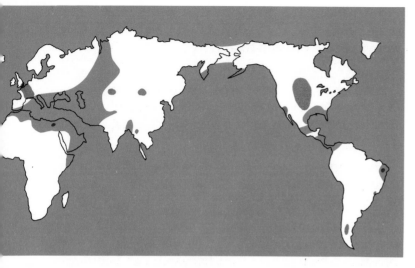

Left: On this map are some of the places where large mammals have been discovered. North America is presumed to have been separate from South America during the Lower Tertiary period, but joined in the far north to Siberia. The land connections between present continents that must have existed then are called land bridges. They made it possible for animals to spread from one part of the world to another. This was how the marsupials managed to reach Australia. When this continent was cut off by the sea, the marsupials were safe from competition with the more advanced kinds of mammal.

One of our distant Eocene ancestors was a tiny, tree-living mammal called a tarsioid. In the Age of Mammals, which has been going on for 70 million years, many forms have become extinct, some evolving into new mammals and others just dying out.

THE HERBIVORES

Most of the mammal giants were plant-eaters or herbivores. Plant-eaters need a greater quantity of food than meat-eaters, hence their larger stomachs and intestines.

Left: *Arsinoitherium*, looking like a huge two-horned rhinoceros, was nearly twelve feet long. Its remains were found in Egypt. This giant also had powerful grinding teeth for chewing plants. Animals like this must have eaten enormous meals every day. Where this monster fits in with other groups of hoofed mammals is not known.

These bulky herbivores, like the elephant and the rhinoceros of today, had strong legs to support their bodies and wide horny nails, or hoofs instead of claws. They are called ungulates, meaning "hoofed" mammals. They also had large molar teeth for grinding up the grass and leaves they fed on.

LIMBS FOR SPEED

Today's mammals are built to move in many different ways – dogs run, monkeys climb, bats fly and whales swim. Yet in spite of this, they have all evolved from common ancestors, going back to the amphibians.

These were the first land vertebrates, and you will remember that they all had similar limbs. There were five toes on each foot, making ten in all.

Most mammals today have far fewer toes and for a good reason. Those that are hunted must move fast in order to escape, so they have evolved long, slender limbs with only a few toes to make contact with the ground.

In a similar way the hunters must move fast on their feet to catch a meal, like a lion after a zebra, or a puma after a deer.

This catching and running away is deadly serious among wild animals. The fastest one of all is the cheetah, which chases speedy gazelles and antelopes. They can all run at speeds of forty (and more) miles an hour.

ODD TOES AND EVEN TOES

The number of toes vary among the ungulates. Some have an even number, like the pigs, deer and sheep, and are called cloven-hoofed. Others have an odd number, like the horse, tapir and rhinoceros. This is very noticeable among the fossil ungulates, and it has helped (together with tooth differences) to sort them into distinct groups. Although they may have looked quite varied, we know which of them belonged to the horse group and so on.

Above: This is the gigantic *Baluchitherium*, one of the large extinct rhinoceroses with long necks. It was about eighteen feet tall and had a head four feet long. With its tall neck it could graze in the tree branches and browse off the leaves, much as the modern giraffe does. Unlike modern rhinoceroses, *Baluchitherium* had no horns.

Right: Here is *Brontotherium,* a huge rhinoceros that had twin horns on its nose. In the picture, it is staring across at *Alticamelus* on the other side of the water.

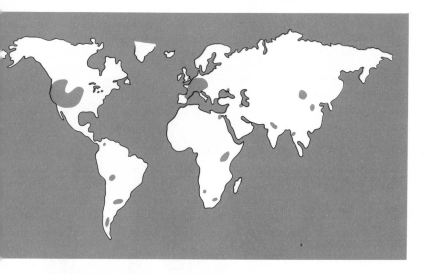

Left: A map showing places where prehistoric mammals have been found from the late Tertiary period. By now South America had joined North America through the Panama "land bridge." This meant that some of the ground sloths and armadillos, which at first lived only in South America, could now move northward. Also, where Alaska and Siberia were still connected across what is now the Bering Sea, slow migrations of horses, rhinos and elephants took place.

RUMINANTS

Many of the larger hoofed mammals have a special way of dealing with their food. It is called "chewing the cud."

If you watch a cow lying in a field you may see its mouth chewing away at something, yet it does not appear to be eating. What has happened is that all the grass it has eaten has already been swallowed, and is stored inside its stomach. This actually has four compartments. In one of these are numerous tiny microbes, called bacteria, which attack the hard substance, called cellulose, which covers grass and softens it to a pulp. This is called the "cud." The

Above: This very strange mammal is called *Moropus,* and was found in America. It had the general build of a clumsy-looking horse, yet there were large claws on its feet. Perhaps these were used for digging the soil in order to feed on roots. This is one of the few examples of a plant-eating mammal which belonged to the ungulates, yet had claws instead of hooves.

67

cow coughs up the cud, chews it and swallows it a second time. Now it can be properly digested in the other chambers of the stomach.

This is very useful for the wild ruminants who must avoid enemies. A deer will steal into the open at dawn or dusk, when conditions appear safe, and quietly feed on grass. It then hides away within the forest, where there is less danger, to chew the cud. If an enemy should approach, it can slip away on its slender legs and disappear among the trees.

The cow in the field is, of course, quite safe, because we protect it from enemies. But, of course, it is descended from wild cud-chewing cattle, which were the prey of meat-eaters.

Ruminants today consist of camels and llamas, deer and giraffes, as well as antelopes, cattle, sheep and goats. They all chew the cud, and all of them have cloven hoofs.

DOMESTIC ANIMALS

Apart from horses and chickens, most of the animals kept on farms and ranches are ruminants, such as cattle, sheep and goats.

These have all been domesticated from wild ancestors, some of which we know about. It all began in the late Stone Age, or Neolithic period, somewhere in the Middle East where Asia joins Europe.

Above: This huge camel is *Alticamelus*, over nine feet tall. Called a "giraffe" camel, it could reach into branches to feed on the leaves. Like a modern camel, it had pads under its feet behind the hooves. Whether or not it had a hump for storing up food like the modern camels of the desert is not known. This prehistoric giant was a forest animal.

Left: *Archaeotherium*, a giant prehistoric pig relative. The first one found came from a coal mine in France. The best-known wild pig today is the wild boar, ancestor of all farm pigs. It lives in the forests of Europe and Asia, and was at one time hunted in countries like Britain, France and Germany.

The ancestor of cattle is thought to be the magnificent giant ox, called *Aurochs* which roamed the forests of Europe and the Near East. It stood six feet high at the shoulders, and was at one time hunted by Stone Age man. He also caught the red deer, which still exists in many places, and looks like the wapiti or elk. Ancient cave paintings of both *aurochs* and red deer have been found in caves in Europe, especially in Lascaux, France.

Below: The giant armadillo relative, *Glyptodon,* was nine feet long. Its strong bony shell was made up of many small pieces fitted together like a jig-saw puzzle. When attacked, it could remain stationary, pull in its head, and wait for danger to pass. *Glyptodons* and sloths lived mainly in South America, although a few managed to reach the southern parts of the United States.

This was one of the animals whose fossil bones were studied by Charles Darwin when he visited South America.

SLOTHS AND ARMADILLOS

When Charles Darwin visited South America as a young man, he was impressed with some large fossil bones that had been discovered in Argentina. They turned out to have belonged to some unusual giants.

One of these, *Glyptodon*, was a kind of giant armadillo measuring nine feet in length. It had a shell on its back, like a tortoise, and could pull in its head and legs, when in danger. Swinging its clubbed tail from side to side must have been an effective defense against enemies.

Giant ground sloths also lived on the plains of South America. Whereas modern sloths are rather small, and spend all their days in the trees, this prehistoric giant, *Megatherium*, meaning the "great beast," lived on the ground. It had very awkward feet with turned-in toes, but it could rear up to reach the branches, and even sit upright by leaning on its tail. It had a long tongue to strip off leaves, as a giraffe does today.

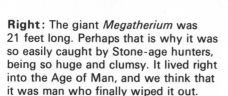

Right: The giant *Megatherium* was 21 feet long. Perhaps that is why it was so easily caught by Stone-age hunters, being so huge and clumsy. It lived right into the Age of Man, and we think that it was man who finally wiped it out.

On the branch is a modern sloth which hangs upside down and feeds on leaves. Sometimes tiny plants grow on its hair in the damp Brazilian jungle, so that it blends with the trees and is difficult to see.

Overleaf: These Siberian mammoths are shoveling snow with their horns as they search for food. You can see a baby mammoth with its mother on the left of the picture, and a woolly rhinoceros on the right.

THE PRIMATES

Our story of prehistoric life is nearly ended. We began with fish, then went on to amphibians, followed by reptiles. Then the mammals expanded, about seventy million years ago, with the opening of the Tertiary period. At that point we mentioned in passing a small tree-climbing creature called a tarsioid. On the right is a picture of a modern tarsier, which looks very much like it.

The tarsioid was a very early example of a mammal with hands. We call these mammals primates, and the group includes tarsiers, bush babies, lemurs, monkeys, apes, and ourselves. We all use our hands for holding onto and picking up things, or even to climb with.

Another thing we have in common is our eyes. These are placed close together in front of the face, so that we see "double". This is called stereoscopic vision. The brain puts the two images together, and this helps us to tell exactly where the doubly seen object is located in space. We can determine just where an object is if we wish to touch it or pick it up. With a monkey it would be most awkward if it were to jump across to another branch only to miss it and tumble down. Being able to judge distance is useful to all primates.

In the story of the primates the tarsioids appeared first. Next came the true monkeys, slightly larger and with better brains. After that, we find apes appearing. Today's apes, like the chimpanzee, are very intelligent. Like us, they have no tails.

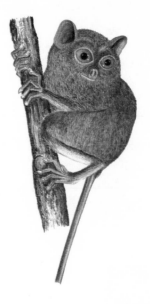

Above: A modern tarsier, a rare and precious "living fossil" still found in the Philippines.

Above: The ring-tailed lemur` is related to the tarsier and is found in Madagascar.

Left: This handsome but dangerous monkey is a male baboon from Africa. It lives among rocks in tribes, and has a "boss" monkey, like this one, to keep order.

Above: The chimpanzee, one of the living apes. The other three are the gorilla, orang-utan, and gibbon. Apes, like ourselves, are close to us on the tree of mammal relationships, but on another branch. We can call them our nearest animal cousins.

MAN APPEARS

Then, much later, it was our turn. About two million years ago there lived some ape-like creatures in Africa that had left the trees and were walking about on the ground. They discovered that sticks and stones were very handy for killing animals and cutting them up. They could also dig up roots and grubs. This was the beginning of the Stone Age, the first age of man.

Because these man-apes, like ourselves, could use their hands for making and using things, we, their human descendants, are called "tool-making animals." Today we are making cars, television sets and space vehicles.

Thus, out of the hundreds of millions of years of animal evolution, man's span so far is only a tiny fraction of time. Hopefully, it is only a beginning.

Right: Among groups of animals where many good fossils have been found it is possible to build up a "family-tree," like this one of elephants. At the bottom is the early Tertiary *Phiomia*. Next comes *Gomphotherium* from a later age, about six feet tall. It had a long snout, but short tusks. Where the arrows separate at the top, the trunked mammal on the right is a mastodon found in North America. All the mastodons became extinct during the Ice Ages. Over on the top left is the well-known woolly mammoth of the Ice Ages, a true elephant like the ones living today in Africa and Asia.

A great deal is known about the mammoth. It was painted on the walls of caves by Stone Age man, over ten thousand years ago. Also, frozen bodies have been found in the cold earth of Siberia and Alaska where the ground never melts. Carcasses with flesh, skin and hair still intact have been found. It has even been possible to trace color in the hair, from which it would seem that the mammoth was auburn in color. At one time it lived as far south as upstate New York.

INDEX

Figures in bold type refer to
illustrations and captions